CONTENTS

ABOUT THE AUTHORS

Alistair Burns, MB ChB, MD, FRCP, FRCPsych, Mphil, DHMSA is Professor of Old Age Psychiatry at the University of Manchester and an Honorary Consultant Old Age Psychiatrist in the Manchester Mental Health Partnership based at Wythenshawe Hospital in South Manchester. He has had clinical and research interests in memory problems and dementia for 15 years and set up the South Manchester Memory Clinic with Sean Page and Jane Winter in 1995. He is editor of the *International Journal of Geriatric Psychiatry* and President-Elect of the International Psychogeriatric Association. He is Director of the North West Dementia Centre.

Sean Page, RMN, MSc is a clinical nurse specialist in old age psychiatry in the Manchester Mental Health Partnership, based at Wythenshawe Hospital in South Manchester. He set up the Memory Clinic in South Manchester in 1995 after running a number of research trials for anti-dementia drugs in South Manchester. He was awarded his MSc from the University of Salford in 1998 based on the role of the nurse in the memory clinic. He is an active advocate of carers and has run successful lectures and courses for carers and other professionals across the North West.

Jane Winter is a consultant clinical psychologist attached to the memory clinic in South Manchester. As well as administering and interpreting neuro-psychological assessments, she is trained in cognitive behaviour therapy. She is currently investigating the technique of errorless learning in patients suffering from Alzheimer's disease.

FOREWORD

More than anything people with dementia and their families need information. They need to understand what is happening to them and prepare for the future. A probable diagnosis of Alzheimer's disease can be frightening and bewildering but information can help us take control of our lives again.

Modern health care also seeks an active partnership between patients, carers and health professionals. Such a partnership cannot come about unless patients and carers are well informed and able to ask questions, challenge the advice they are given and make informed choices. There are now a wide range of sources of information and advice, not least through the internet, but we need to have confidence in the reliability and accuracy of the information we are given. That is where this book makes a valuable contribution. Its authors are experienced and knowledgeable and bring perspectives from psychiatry, psychology and nursing.

Alzheimer's Disease and Memory Loss Explained puts the range of conditions causing memory loss into perspective. It describes the different types of dementia, how they may be diagnosed and the many things that can be done to treat the symptoms and maintain quality of life. It deals sensibly with the new drug treatments and also with treatment approaches which do not involve drugs. It is particularly informative about the early stages of the disease and how people with dementia can look after themselves.

This book will be useful to family members, but also to doctors, to care workers, to nurses and other health professionals who want to know more about one of the growing health challenges of our time.

Harry Cayton OBE
Chief Executive, Alzheimer's Society

PREFACE

The idea of this book was stimulated by the need to provide more information to people about memory loss, ageing, dementia and Alzheimer's disease. It grew out of our clinical work in the memory clinic in South Manchester where the desire to keep our patients, their carers and relatives fully informed of what we do and why we do it has always been uppermost in our minds. The book is aimed at a number of different groups of people. Primarily it is for people without a professional training in the field who wish to know more about these common problems. We think that anyone who has been referred to a clinic might be interested in reading it, as would their relatives and friends. A person who has noticed that their memory is not what it used to be and wants to know about the possible significance of the symptoms may find it of help, as indeed might someone who knows someone else with a poor memory. Finally, we hope it could be read (perhaps even enjoyed) by anybody who is curious about memory loss, the effects of ageing on memory, dementia, or who has simply heard about Alzheimer's disease and wants to know more. We are grateful to our patients and their relatives who have provided us with a reason to write about this most important subject. This publication would not have been possible without the help and support of Barbara Dignan, our secretary, and Peter Altman, our publisher. We are grateful to Richard Burns, Janet Burns and Professor David Harnden for commenting on early drafts of the manuscript.

Alistair Burns
Sean Page
Jane Winter

Manchester
2001

1 INTRODUCTION

What is memory?

Memory is the ability to recall past experience or knowledge. It is, of course, not something that relates only to humans – cats and dogs remember where they live, rats can be trained to remember which part of a maze contains food, birds remember where their nests are, etc.

Some people have better memories than others and this is just the normal variation that one sees in large groups of people. A few seem to have exceptional powers of memory in that they can remember many objects at short notice, such as the order of shuffled packs of cards. However, this isn't quite what it seems, as certain techniques are used to help the performer recall the items.

Short-term and long-term memory

Memory can be divided into short-term memory and long-term memory. Short-term memory deals with anything that is remembered over a few minutes, such as the colour of a car that you have just seen turn a corner; and long-term memory is anything that is remembered for a longer time, such as your address. Everything to be committed to memory passes through short-term memory to reach long-term memory. The process in which items in short-term memory are put into long-term memory is called **storage**. The reverse, when they are brought out of long-term memory back into short-term memory is called **retrieval**.

Long-term memory is divided into three types.

Type of Memory	Examples	Comments
Procedural memory	Riding a bicycle Playing the piano	Done almost without thinking
Semantic memory	The capital of England	Knowledge that has been acquired but we cannot recall exactly when
Episodic memory	Someone's name or phone number	Personal memories of everyday life

When we remember things, we retrieve them out of long-term memory. If we say we forget something, this could be a difficulty in the laying down of memory in the first place, known as **encoding**, the storing of memory (storage), or pulling it out of long-term memory (retrieval). Thus, forgetting somebody's name may be due to the fact that when a person was introduced, one did not encode or store the information appropriately. Alternatively, if the information was stored, it may be a failure of retrieval – this is the basis of the phrase 'on the tip of my tongue'.

Memory and the brain

For those readers who are interested, this paragraph gives some information about which parts of the brain are involved in memory. Figure 1.1 shows the major brain areas that are concerned with memory. There are two areas that seem to have a major role to play. The first is the temporal lobe, and the three structures within it. These are the hippocampus (a horseshoe-shaped structure in the middle of the brain) and two adjacent structures, the subiculum and dentate gyrus, which are connected with the hippocampus. The hippocampus seems particularly associated with the laying down of new memories. The amygdala, which lies adjacent to the hippocampus, seems to be concerned with emotional aspects of memory. The middle part of the brain, the diencephalon, has two main structures, the thalamus and the mammillary bodies. A specific type of memory loss occurs in people who have been alcoholics for a number of years and have a deficiency of thiamine (vitamin B1). Bleeding occurs in the mammillary bodies and a particularly dense amnesia occurs. Secondly, the frontal lobes of the brain appear to have a role in preservation of memory. This is in addition to their better known function of regulating our personalities and protecting us from being disinhibited. (People with damage to the frontal lobe are often disinhibited and lack the usual social control that governs behaviour.)

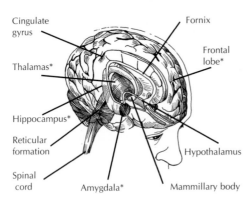

Cingulate gyrus

Fornix

Thalamas*

Frontal lobe*

Hippocampus*

Reticular formation

Hypothalamus

Spinal cord

Amygdala*

Mammillary body

Figure 1.1 The human brain revealed. Structures labelled with an asterisk are known to be involved in memory in that when they are damaged they can give rise to a profound amnesia.

What is dementia?

Dementia is a condition in which there is a serious deterioration in a person's intellectual ability and emotional state. It can be due to a number of different causes and, although the end result may appear to be the same to a lay person, the treatment and the progression of the illness vary according to the cause. It is therefore very important for a doctor to know the type of dementia from which a person suffers, and tests and examinations can be carried out to find the cause.

Dementia defines the presence of a certain set of symptoms and signs.

A symptom is something that a patient complains of – for example, a pain, or constipation. A sign is something that a doctor notices or uncovers on a clinical examination – for example, raised blood pressure or an abnormal heartbeat. A syndrome is a condition that has a recognisable number of signs and symptoms. Dementia is an example of a syndrome.

The two commonest causes of dementia are Alzheimer's disease and vascular dementia. Alzheimer's disease is caused by the presence of abnormal proteins in the brain, which interfere with the proper functioning of the brain by disturbing the way in which the brain cells communicate with each other. It is not known why this abnormal protein appears. About 60% of people with dementia have Alzheimer's disease. Vascular dementia is caused by hardening of the blood vessels in the brain, which results in poor blood flow to the brain and damage (and sometimes death) of brain cells. About 20% of people with dementia have vascular dementia. Alzheimer's disease and vascular dementia can both exist in the same person.

The two less common types of dementia are:
• Lewy body dementia, which is caused by an abnormal protein deposit between the nerve cells (similar to but not the same as the protein deposited in Alzheimer's disease); and
• frontal lobe dementia, which is caused by a specific shrinkage of cells in the front part of the brain, resulting in change in a person's personality and behaviour.

Summary

Causes of dementia
• Alzheimer's disease: 60%
• Vascular dementia: 20%
• Lewy body dementia: 15%

• Other causes (such as frontal lobe dementia, brain tumours, vitamin deficiency, hydrocephalus): 5%

Symptoms and signs of dementia

These can be described under three headings:
• loss of memory and higher brain functions (such as carrying out complex tasks such as driving, doing crosswords and planning activities);
• psychiatric symptoms and behavioural disturbances; and
• activities of daily living.

Loss of memory and higher brain functions
Loss of memory occurs in all people with Alzheimer's disease. It is often the first symptom and gradually gets worse. Often others notice someone's memory loss first. It may be that someone forgets a birthday or an anniversary or begins to forget appointments. Of course, these can be normal experiences, particularly as people get older, but if they are severe, and most importantly, if they get worse over time, that is suggestive that someone may have a dementia. People's

judgement can become impaired and they find it progressively more difficult to make complex and important decisions. They can find it increasingly difficult to handle their own affairs, particularly their financial affairs. People can also have problems understanding language and expressing themselves, sometimes have difficulty in recognising other people and, when the dementia is severe, they need help to wash, dress and feed themselves. The symptoms of memory loss have to be interpreted in the light of a person's age. Forgetting appointments and names in a 70-year-old man would be of less significance than the same losses in a 50-year-old man.

Psychiatric symptoms and behavioural disturbances
There are a whole host of psychiatric and psychological symptoms and disturbances in behaviour that accompany dementia. The common ones are:
• depression: this is very common and about a third of people with dementia have significant depression. In addition, it is known that an episode of depression earlier in life is a risk factor for the development of Alzheimer's disease.
• delusions: these are fixed ideas which are usually false but are held intensively and a person cannot be dissuaded from them. In dementia, common delusions are that people have stolen a person's possessions or that people wish to annoy or harm the sufferer.
• other symptoms: these include hallucinations (seeing things or hearing things).
• behavioural disturbances: there are many types of behavioural disturbance such as aggression (this can be verbal aggression, such as shouting and screaming or physical aggression such as hitting or punching), agitation (where a person appears very restless and is unable to sit contentedly and at peace) and wandering (a person may walk out of their own home, forget where they are and walk for miles, or if a person is in a nursing or residential home, they may walk around the home constantly).

Activities of daily living
The final expression of dementia is where people are unable to look after themselves and complete, without help, what are called activities of daily living. These are things like getting dressed, going to the toilet, brushing one's teeth, combing one's hair and eating a meal. In the early stages of dementia, problems with activities of daily living may be shown by an inability to carry out tasks such as shopping independently, using the telephone, handling money and driving. It is a popular misconception to assume that a person with dementia has simply 'forgotten' how to do these things. The situation is more complex and to carry out these tasks the brain needs to do more than simply remember how they were carried out the last time.

Summary

Signs of dementia
- Memory loss
- Forgetfulness
- Disorientation to time and place
- Personality changes
- Problems shopping and using the telephone
- Difficulty dressing and washing
- Hallucinations
- Delusions
- Depression

Definition of terms

Activities of daily living: things which we carry out in our everyday lives and which are affected in someone suffering from dementia. Examples include dressing, feeding, washing, eating, handling money, shopping, driving and using the telephone

Alzheimer's disease: the commonest cause of dementia affecting about 60% of people with dementia

Anticholinesterase drugs: a new type of drug that improves the symptoms of Alzheimer's disease by raising the level of a neurotransmitter, acetylcholine, in the brain

Behavioural disturbances: behaviours such as wandering, agitation, aggression and sexual disinhibition seen in people with dementia

Cognitive function: memory, language and mental agility

Confusion: a state in which a person does not know where they are and/or does not know the date, and/or does things that are inappropriate

Court of protection: an official part of the court system which protects a person who, through dementia or any other mental illness, has lost the ability to handle their affairs

CT scan: a type of brain scan that shows the structure of the brain

Delirium: a state indicated by a sudden onset of brain dysfunction and characterised by florid symptoms and fluctuation in conscious level. Caused by a physical illness upsetting normal brain function

Delusions: false ideas that are fixed and unshakable and often seen in people with dementia

Dementia: a condition of the brain, with a number of causes which gives rise to memory loss, emotion changes and results in a person having difficulties looking after him/herself

Depression: a state of lowered mood seen commonly in people with dementia

Frontal lobe dementia: a type of dementia caused by shrinkage in the front part of the brain

Hallucinations: experiences such as visual or auditory hallucinations (seeing or hearing things when there is nothing there) seen in people with dementia

Lewy body dementia: a type of dementia caused by deposits of protein called Lewy bodies in the brain

Memory clinic: an outpatient clinic specialising in the diagnosis and treatment of people with memory disorders

Misidentifications: when a person with dementia does not recognise a person or an object

MRI scan: another type of brain scan that shows the structure of the brain in finer detail compared to a CT scan

Neuropsychiatric features: psychiatric or psychological symptoms and behavioural disturbances seen in dementia

Neuropsychological features: part of the expression of dementia characterised by amnesia (loss of memory), aphasia (problems understanding or expressing words), agnosia (failure to recognise people or objects), and apraxia (the inability to carry out tasks such as writing, dressing or using a knife and fork

Neurotransmitter: a chemical substance in the brain, which allows messages to be sent from one brain cell (neurone) to another

Psychiatric symptoms: symptoms such as depression, delusions, hallucinations and misidentification seen in people with dementia

Psychotic symptoms: symptoms such as delusions, hallucinations and misidentifications

Vascular dementia: the second commonest cause of dementia affecting about 20% of people with dementia

2 DIAGNOSIS AND ASSESSMENT OF DEMENTIA

As stated in Chapter 1, it is important to discover the cause of dementia. To say that someone has dementia simply describes what is seen. It is like saying that somebody has back pain. The important thing is to discover the cause of the dementia, and not simply to describe the fact that it is there. However, to start with, the doctor needs to be sure that the patient is actually suffering from dementia and not from just, say, depression. At first glance, a depressed patient may appear to be demented, but this is not necessarily the case. A series of tests and investigations is carried out in order to arrive at a proper diagnosis. The following conditions and situations all need to be considered.

Confounding factors

Depression

Depression is a common illness and affects many elderly people. There are two types. The first is severe and usually needs treatment from a doctor or psychologist – it is often referred to as a clinical depression. On average, 3 or 4% of the population will have clinical depression at any one time, but the percentage affected will vary widely depending upon the group examined, e.g. there will be variation between younger and older groups. Clinical depression is different from another type of depression, which is milder and affects up to 20% of people. The symptoms in this type of depression (sometimes called minor or subclinical depression) are relatively mild, they do not last very long, and tend not to distress or concern people. This type of depression usually does not need to be treated and is self-limiting, although some people's symptoms may progress to become a clinical depression.

Some of the symptoms of depression are similar to those of people with dementia. People who are depressed often complain of a poor memory and say that they lack concentration. These symptoms also occur in people with dementia. To make things more complicated, depression can occur in people suffering from dementia. Some people say that this is a natural reaction when a person begins to realise that their memory is failing. When someone goes to the doctor with signs and symptoms of dementia, a careful examination of that person's mental state is needed to decide whether they are depressed or not. If there is any doubt, most doctors would err on the side of caution and give people a course of antidepressants (a so-called 'treatment trial') and assess whether they get better or not.

Normal ageing

Memory lapses are common as we get older and can occur if a person has a great deal on their mind or is trying to do too many things. However, the fact that a person has come along and asked for help suggests they are bothered by it. The way in which dementia is tested for is to carry out tests of cognitive function (tests of memory and other things like language). If you take a representative group of people and carry out a memory test, you get what is called 'a normal distribution' of scores. In that way, it is like height and weight – some people are taller than others, some people are lighter than others – some people have scores at either end, some low and some high, but the vast majority of people score in the middle. This has led some people to say that dementia is not really an illness, it just represents one end of a spectrum. It is not like cancer, which you either have or do not have. Things are not as clear cut in relation to dementia, but there is no doubt that it is possible to identify a group of people who score very badly on tests of cognitive function who are bothered by their memory and who turn out to have dementia.

Poor performance in tests of cognitive function is only one part of how dementia is expressed. There are other aspects of the disorder (problems with activities of daily living, poor judgement and psychiatric symptoms) which are needed to make a diagnosis of dementia, and these do not normally occur in the absence of the disease. Memory loss can occur at any age. A certain degree of loss can be expected as people get older. For example, minor lapses of memory do not need to concern people in their eighties but would be of more significance in someone of 40.

Delirium
In older people, delirium is caused by a physical illness and this seems to produce a chemical imbalance in the brain, which gives rise to symptoms of confusion. The person has trouble thinking and can appear disorientated (i.e. they do not know where they are and do not know the date, month, year or season). The best way of discriminating delirium from dementia is to enquire how the illness started and how it progressed. In dementia, the illness tends to start slowly and progress slowly, whereas in delirium it starts quickly and the symptoms tend to fluctuate from day to day. Also, in delirium there is almost always a physical cause for the symptoms (an infection in the chest or in the urine, heart failure, and cancer are common causes of delirium). The situation is complicated by the fact that people who have dementia, if they become physically ill, are more prone to getting an episode of delirium as well.

Drugs
All drugs have unwanted side-effects. People with dementia are probably more prone to suffer from a physical illness and are, generally speaking, more likely to get side-effects from medication. This is especially true if a person is taking more than one drug. A doctor will always consider carefully the drugs a person is taking. Sometimes, stopping a drug for a short time can be helpful in deciding whether it is contributing to, or may be causing, symptoms related to dementia.

8

Learning disability (mental handicap)

Dementia is something which people may develop at some point during their life, i.e. it is not something a person is born with. People suffering from learning disability have often had their condition since birth and it has led to a lifelong impairment in cognitive functioning. It can be very difficult to assess if a person with learning disability has developed a dementia as the diagnosis rests on demonstrating a change in cognitive function. People with learning disability (particularly Down's syndrome) can develop dementia later in life, and often the manifestations of that dementia are more apparent in terms of abnormal behaviour rather than symptoms or complaints of memory loss. There is a specific association between Down's syndrome and Alzheimer's disease in that the majority of patients with Down's syndrome develop, after the age of 40 years, structural changes in their brains similar to those seen in Alzheimer's disease.

The effects of poor environmental stimulation

Many of the tests that are used to assess dementia need co-operation and a person has to have a certain degree of initiative, education, and general intelligence to be able to respond normally to them. Occasionally people who have lived in a very unstimulating environment for many years (for example, in an institution) will perform poorly on tests and may give the impression that they have dementia. However, these situations are rare. One example would be people who, for some reason, have lived in a long-stay hospital for a long time without much contact with the outside world and not much stimulation. These individuals can appear to have dementia, so the environment in which a person lives must be taken into account when carrying out an assessment.

Poor eyesight and vision

Tests of cognitive function need a person, generally, to have good eyesight and satisfactory hearing to be completed successfully. In people who are totally blind and/or totally deaf, it can be hard to assess their memory. Minor problems with eyesight and hearing can easily be remedied with glasses and a hearing aid.

Summary
Things that can be mistaken for dementia and affect its diagnosis

- Depression
- Normal ageing
- Learning disability
- Delirium (due to physical illness)
- Poor environmental stimulation
- Poor eyesight and poor hearing

Differential diagnosis of the cause of the dementia

Once a diagnosis of dementia has been made, the next stage is to assess its cause. A series of tests and examinations are carried out to exclude diseases in the rest of the body, some of which are treatable, and to rule out some other brain conditions. When this has been done, the doctor will decide whether the cause is Alzheimer's disease, vascular dementia (or a combination of the two), dementia of Lewy body type, dementia of frontal lobe type or one of the other causes.

Illnesses in the rest of the body

There are a number of different illnesses that appear to affect the brain in ways that can cause symptoms similar to dementia. People who have an underactive thyroid gland can have problems with poor concentration and poor memory. Often there are other signs of an underactive thyroid, such as tiredness, dislike of cold weather, weight gain, thinning of the hair or sometimes an enlarged thyroid gland, a goitre. It can be detected by a simple blood test and replacement treatment with the hormone is easily given in the form of a tablet.

People who have particular deficiencies of certain vitamins can also have symptoms of a dementia. Too little vitamin B_{12} and folic acid can give rise to symptoms of dementia, particularly if the deficiencies are very severe. These deficiencies can sometimes arise because of a bad diet. It is complicated because some people who have dementia from other causes can neglect their diet and get low levels of these vitamins. Treatment is in the form of tablets for folic acid and injections for vitamin B_{12}.

Any general physical illness can give rise to symptoms of dementia, which is why a person with suspected dementia will have a general physical examination and blood test to make sure that medical conditions such as anaemia, liver and kidney problems, diabetes and raised cholesterol in the blood are detected and treated.

Changes within the brain

People may develop brain tumours, which can give rise to symptoms of dementia. The symptoms of a brain tumour are often physical, e.g. headache or a feeling of sickness, particularly in the morning. They may well have other physical symptoms such as loss of muscle power, or tingling, in an arm or leg. There are several types of brain tumours, some arising in the brain itself, and others where the tumour has started somewhere else in the body and smaller parts have spread to the brain. Bleeding may occur in the outer covers of the brain, especially after a head injury (bleeding inside the brain gives a stroke).

Brain tumours and bleeding can be detected on a brain scan and can therefore be distinguished from the main types of dementia. If someone has had a severe head injury and the clinical symptoms have come on quite suddenly afterwards, one might suspect that a bleed in the brain has taken place. Repeated head injuries give rise to a form of dementia, found in boxers, called 'dementia

10

pugilistica' or Punch Drunk Syndrome.

The other main type of problem which can occur in the brain is called 'hydrocephalus' (literally, water on the brain). What happens normally is that the fluid which bathes the brain inside the skull (the cerebrospinal fluid) flows inside the brain and then out through a narrow channel to the outside surface of the brain and down the spinal cord, where it is absorbed into the bloodstream. This fluid is very important in protecting the brain against injury. When there is a blockage to the flow of the fluid from the inside of the brain to the outside, the pressure builds up inside, and the areas inside the brain are forced outwards and upwards by the pressure of fluid, causing the symptoms of hydrocephalus. This can occur in some people after a very severe infection of the brain or a type of bleed in the brain which takes place in the outer surface, called a subarachnoid haemorrhage. In children, because the skull bones have not fused together, there is space with this increasing pressure for the head to get bigger. However, very early on in life the skull binds together and the increase in pressure merely squashes the brain. It is an important condition to identify, because it can be treated by inserting a tube inside the brain to relieve the pressure.

Alzheimer's disease

This is the commonest cause of dementia and affects about 60% of people who suffer from dementia. It is called Alzheimer's disease after the doctor, Alois Alzheimer, who first described it in 1907. He was both a psychiatrist and pathologist and described the case of a woman who died when she was aged 51 and had all the symptoms of dementia. She had a post-mortem examination and her brain was examined under the microscope. Dr Alzheimer found two abnormalities: layers of protein in between the nerve cells (called neuritic plaques) and areas of damaged nerve fibres which, instead of being straight, had become tangled (called neurofibrillary tangles). He described the case in a medical journal and in 1910, his teacher (a psychiatrist called Emil Kraepelin) wrote a book and named the disease after his pupil, Alzheimer. Because Alzheimer had described his disease in a young person (aged 51), Alzheimer's disease became recognised as a cause of dementia at younger ages – called a pre-senile dementia. The outdated and pejorative term 'senile dementia' was reserved for older people who became confused and forgetful (there was an arbitrary cut-off between senile and pre-senile at aged 65). It was regarded that older people who developed senile dementia (in common language became senile) had a form of hardening of the arteries or arthrosclerosis. Alzheimer's disease was regarded as a disease of younger people and not older people.

In the late 1960s and 1970s a series of studies in Newcastle in the UK correlated the clinical symptoms of older people with dementia with the changes in their brains after they had died. They showed that older people did, in fact, suffer from Alzheimer's disease much more commonly than was once thought and so over the next decade it became fully appreciated that Alzheimer's disease was the commonest type of dementia affecting older people. The term senile dementia with all its negative associations was dropped.

It is obviously unethical and impractical to carry out a brain biopsy on everyone who is suspected of having Alzheimer's disease and so a number of studies have looked at a particular set of clinical symptoms and signs, the results of a number of post-mortem investigations on individuals after the person has died. This has led to the development of so called 'diagnostic criteria', which are a set of guidelines. If they are all satisfied, then we know there is a very high chance (over 90%) that somebody has Alzheimer's disease. For example, a person who has dementia, whose illness has started slowly and has progressed gradually, has no signs of stroke or risk factors for stroke, on blood tests shows no evidence of thyroid deficiency or vitamin deficiency or no other abnormalities, and whose CT scan does not reveal any intracranial bleeding or brain tumour, can be assumed with over 90% confidence to be suffering from Alzheimer's disease. In this way, a clinician can make an accurate diagnosis without the need to examine the pathological changes in the brain. Of course, as new tests and examinations are invented, these criteria are being updated all the time. Similar criteria exist for the other types of dementia.

Possible signs of Alzheimer's disease
Problems with any of these activities
Memory problems
- Forgetting people's names?
- Forgetting appointments?
- Forgetting conversations you have had with people?
- Forgetting where you have put things?
- Tending to repeat yourself?
- Having trouble paying attention?

Handling complex tasks
- Difficulty cooking a meal or organising for your bills to be paid?
- Trouble working new pieces of equipment that you or your family have bought?
- More trouble adding things up in your head than you used to?
- Crossword taking longer to do than it used to?

Reasoning ability
- Tending to get flustered in new situations?
- Having difficulty in solving everyday problems that you used to solve without a second thought; for example, knowing what to do if the lights in the house fused?

Disorientation
- Getting lost on what are familiar routes?
- Getting lost when you are driving?
- Forgetting what day it is and having to ask somebody?

Behaviour
- Being more irritable than usual?
- People commenting that a change in personality seems to have occurred?
- Less easy-going than you used to be?

[It is very common, particularly as we get older, to have lapses of memory. Remember – if you forget somebody's name, it doesn't mean you have Alzheimer's disease. All these things happen occasionally to people – it is only if they are common (perhaps more than once a month), and/or if they are getting more frequent that you may need to seek help.]

Vascular dementia
This form of dementia can be caused by a stroke. In the 1970s it was considered that to have vascular dementia you needed at least one or two big strokes. However, it has become apparent over the last 20 years that people can have vascular dementia without having had strokes. Even if someone has a stroke, it does not necessarily give rise to any symptoms of dementia, and it can often be found as an incidental finding on a brain scan, or even recognised only after someone has died, at post-mortem examination. It is important to differentiate people with vascular dementia from people with Alzheimer's disease, because the treatment is very different. There are a few tell-tale signs that people may have vascular dementia rather than Alzheimer's disease. The symptoms tend to start very quickly and tend to vary from day to day. At times, people will say that a relative appears to be back to normal. There may be a history of a stroke or a transient ischaemic attack (i.e. a mini-stroke where the symptoms last less than 24 hours). A person may have a history of high blood pressure or heart disease, raised cholesterol, or diabetes.

Lewy body dementia
This describes a particular type of dementia, characterised by:
- episodes of delirium (i.e. brief episodes of deterioration in memory);
- falls;
- symptoms of Parkinson's disease (when symptoms of Parkinson's disease are present but a person is not considered to have the disease, they are called Parkinsonian symptoms – the commonest ones are mild tremor at rest, and stiffness of the muscles);
- a number of psychiatric symptoms, such as paranoid ideas (the idea that someone is trying to harm or come after the individual), and visual hallucinations (when someone sees something but there is nobody and nothing there);
- an exaggerated reaction to neuroleptic drugs which cause stiffness of the muscles.

The disease is named after the pathologist who described deposits of protein between nerve cells in the brain similar to the protein described by Alzheimer.

Interestingly, when these areas of protein are found in a central region of the brain (called the basal ganglia), the patient will have the symptoms of Parkinson's disease. It is important to make a diagnosis of Lewy body dementia, because some of the drugs that are given to people with dementia to control troublesome symptoms, such as agitation and aggression, can provoke a very severe reaction in people with Lewy body dementia.

Frontal lobe dementia
This is where the front parts of the brain are affected by shrinkage of unknown cause. Symptoms here are slightly different in that changes in personality are very obvious, and sometimes the person can have problems with language. Memory tends not to be affected very early on. People with this disease can behave quite bizarrely at times.

Creutzfeldt–Jakob disease
This has hit the headlines recently because of its association with BSE (bovine spongiform encephalopathy). The illness usually progresses very rapidly (some may die within a year or 18 months). Patients may have myoclonic jerks (a sudden muscular spasm affecting the body). An electroencephalogram (EEG) shows a characteristically abnormal pattern. A blood test is available with specialist advice.

Summary
Causes of dementia
- Changes inside the brain
  Water on the brain
  (hydrocephalus)
  Bleeding in the coverings
  of the brain
  Brain tumours

- Physical illness
- Alzheimer's disease
- Vascular dementia
- Lewy body dementia
- Frontal lobe dementia

Investigation of a person suspected of having dementia

There is a fairly set routine which is followed when someone suspected of having dementia attends their general practitioner or a specialist clinic. A number of memory clinics are in existence in the UK. They are usually attached to departments of Old Age Psychiatry or Geriatric Medicine and specialise in the diagnosis and treatment of people with memory problems, whatever their age. They are becoming increasingly recognised as one of the most effective ways to encourage the early diagnosis and management of memory loss. Contrary to popular belief and expectation, a diagnosis of dementia and its causes is relatively straightforward. Many people have great faith in expensive brain scans but for many people this is not necessary. Of course, there are situations where the diagnosis is particularly difficult or complex and further investigations are needed, but generally they are not. It is generally sufficient to examine the patient and take a clinical history. The main points of the history and examination are outlined below.

History of the illness

Patients are usually well able to describe their own symptoms, how they started and how they have developed, but if someone has a significant degree of memory loss, disorientation, confusion or dementia, it is necessary to take the history almost entirely from a relative or carer. Even if the patient is able to describe his or her symptoms accurately, it is always important to check the history with someone else. The types of question that are asked are:

- When did the symptoms start?
- What was the first symptom?
- Did it start suddenly or gradually?
- Has it progressed suddenly or gradually?
- Were there any special circumstances around the time the symptoms started?
- Is there anything that has made them worse or better?
- What is the person's reaction to the symptoms?
- Have other people outside the family noticed anything?

A doctor or nurse will often ask some specific questions about particular symptoms from which a patient with dementia might suffer. These would include specific symptoms about depression. For example:

- Have you been feeling very tired recently?
- Do you find your concentration is poor?
- Do you look forward to the future?
- Do you feel guilty about anything?
- Do you enjoy things?
- Do you sleep well at night?
- Have you lost weight?
- Is there any change in your mood during the day? (for example, feeling worse in the morning)
- Have other people said you have been more irritable recently?

It might be appropriate to ask specific questions about delusions and other psychiatric symptoms. It is also important to get an idea what the person can and cannot do in terms of activities of daily living:

- Can they still do the shopping on their own?
- Are they able to handle money?
- Can they still drive safely?
- Are they still as neat and tidy as they used to be?
- Do they comb their hair as much as they used to?
- Do they need to be reminded to change their clothes?

Examination of the mental state

This consists of questions concerning how a person is feeling and is to check out whether an individual is depressed or has any psychotic ideas or experiences. If a person complains of a physical illness, then it is necessary to ask some specific questions about physical symptoms.

When someone is suspected of having dementia, the most important part of the examination is a test of memory function. Other areas to test are language, a person's ability to follow commands, to write and to draw. Taken altogether, these are referred to as 'cognitive functions'. There are a number of standard tests that are available or the doctor or nurse might just ask some general questions without recording them in a formal scale. Generally people favour recording memory problems in a formal way.

The most popular test is the Mini-Mental State Examination. It consists of 20 questions and gives a score out of 30 (some of the questions carry more than one mark). It takes about 10 minutes to complete. Some examples of questions used to test cognitive function are as follows:

- *Orientation to time and place.* The person is asked to say the date (the day of the week, the month, the year, the season and the date in the month), and also where the person is (does the person know what city or town they are in, do they know their address at home, do they know the district they are in or do they know the name of the hospital they are in?).
- *Memory.* It is important to do a test of memory. Generally this consists of asking a person to repeat three words straight after the interviewer and then the person is asked them again a minute or two later. This tests both immediate memory (registration of memory) and long-term memory (after 1 or 2 minutes). This specific test of memory does not relate to what people generally regard as short- and long-term memory (i.e. things that have happened in the past day or the past week are short-term memory and things that happened 30 or 40 years ago are long-term memory). Examples of words used in the test include 'ball', 'car', 'man', 'apple', 'table' and 'penny'.
- *Concentration.* There is usually a test of concentration. This can take two forms. Often someone is asked to spell a word backwards, after spelling it forwards. Alternatively, someone is asked to take 7 away from 100 and tell the interviewer each number they get (i.e. the person would say, 93, 86, 79, 72, 65 – the person is generally stopped at that point). It is often important to get an idea if the person can tell the interviewer anything that is happening in the news.
- *Language function.* This is tested by asking a person to name a common object such as a watch, a pen, a tie or a pair of shoes.
- *Copying.* There is often a test to measure if a person can copy a figure. This can be a simple figure such as a triangle or a more complex one such as two intersecting five-sided figures.
- *Following instructions.* The person may also be asked to carry out a simple command such as to take a piece of paper in their right hand, fold it in half and put it on the floor.

• *Clock drawing test.* A test which is becoming more popular is when a person is asked to draw a clock. This can take a number of forms. For example, when the person is asked to draw a clock face which includes drawing a circle and putting the numbers in, and then putting the hands to show a time, such as 10 past 10. This is a test of how a particular part of the brain is working.

In specialist settings, more detailed neuropsychological tests are carried out. These can only be given by specially trained psychology staff and can take anything up to an hour. They provide a very thorough picture of how the brain is functioning.

Physical examination
This takes the form of a general physical examination, which would include checking the pulse and blood pressure, listening to the heart and lungs, and testing the reflexes to see if there are any signs of a stroke. In practice this means tapping with a tendon hammer on the elbows, wrists, ankle and knees. A key is often drawn along the base of the foot to see in which direction the big toe moves (if it moves down it is normal, if it moves up it suggests a person may have had a stroke). The strength of muscles in the arms and legs is also tested – weakness may indicate that there has been a stroke. A test of coordination may be performed, such as asking a person to touch their own nose with their index finger and then touch the examiner's finger and then do it repeatedly.

Physical investigations
These usually include the following:
• a blood test – this is subjected to a routine analysis which includes a full blood count (to check there is no anaemia);
• tests of liver function and kidney function;
• blood glucose;
• tests of level of thyroid hormone in the blood and vitamin levels (vitamin B_{12} and folic acid).

A urine sample is often taken to test for evidence of any sugar in the urine or any infections.

A chest x-ray is carried out if the person has symptoms of chest disease, whilst a tracing of the heart (electrocardiogram, ECG) is carried out if the person has heart symptoms. A tracing of the brain waves (electroencephalogram, EEG) is useful since it gives one more information about the function of the brain's activity. It can show if a person is likely to have a delirium or if they have had a stroke.

Usually, if someone is suspected of having dementia, a brain scan is carried out. There are two common types of brain scan. A computed tomography (or computed axial tomography) scan is the commonest. This is known as a CT scan or CAT scan. This is a non-invasive procedure and can be carried out in about 5 or 10 minutes. It involves lying on a movable bed and putting your head in what looks like a large washing machine or dishwasher. Modern scanners tend not to be as enclosed or claustrophobic as older scanners. Occasionally, there may be a need for an injection, which can highlight areas of the brain. The main reason for carrying out a CT or CAT scan is that it can show the structure of the brain. If there is a tumour or clot or haemorrhage, this can be seen. If there is shrinkage of the brain, this can be seen as well and it is sometimes helpful to know if one part of the brain is more shrunken than another part.

A second type of brain scan is called an MRI or magnetic resonance imaging scan, which uses a slightly different technique from that of the CT scan. Because the head is put in a magnet, there are some situations where someone could not have an MRI scan – for example, if they have had a previous operation in their brain and a metal clip has been placed on an artery, or if they have a cardiac pacemaker. Also, the apparatus for an MRI scan is much more confining and anyone who suffers from claustrophobia might become anxious or nervous.

Both scans are painless. A CT scan takes about 5 minutes and an MRI scan about 20 minutes but the time can vary significantly. Examples of scans are shown in Figures 2.1–2.7.

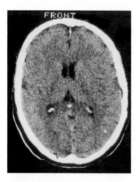

Figure 2.1 A picture of a normal brain taken looking down from above. The white circle around the outside is the skull, the grey material is the brain itself, and the black areas are the fluid (cerebrospinal fluid) that bathes the brain. The white line going down at the top of the brain is a band of fibres containing calcium that separates the two halves. The three white areas just below the centre are deposits of calcium. The black area just above that is just space inside the brain, and is called the ventricle. As can be seen, the grey area goes right up to the skull, showing that there is no shrinkage of the brain. The thin, horizontal white line at the top of the picture was caused by the patient moving during the scan.

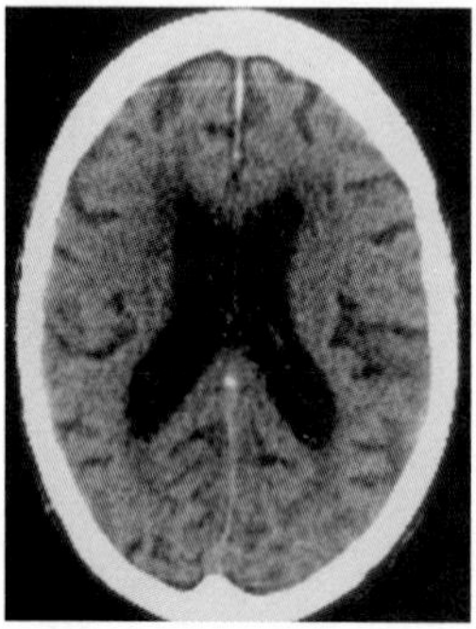

Figure 2.2 This is a picture of the brain showing that the areas of cerebrospinal fluid inside the brain (the ventricles) are greatly enlarged. This suggests that the inside of the brain adjacent to the ventricle has shrunk. Also, there are black lines throughout the grey brain substance showing that the brain has shrunk and has been replaced by cerebrospinal fluid.

18

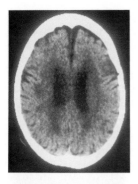

Figure 2.3 A picture of a brain showing the ventricles in the middle with a fuzzy appearance. This shows that there is some blood vessel disease in the brain, which is caused by a hardening of the arteries. At the 2 o'clock position, the black area next to the skull represents damaged brain tissue due to a cut–off of the blood supply, resulting in a stroke. At the 12 o'clock position, the space between the two halves of the brain is very wide, suggesting that there has been shrinkage at the front.

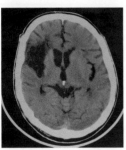

Figure 2.4 A picture of a brain showing a massive area of damage at the 10 o'clock position.

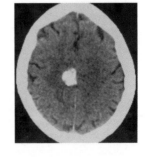

Figure 2.5 This shows a brain tumour, made up of calcium growing in the midline of the brain.

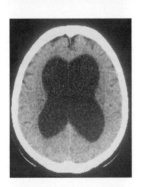

Figure 2.6 This is an example of normal pressure hydrocephalus. The ventricles in the middle of the brain are huge. There is no evidence of shrinkage of the brain on the outside (i.e. there are no black areas between the edge of the brain and the white rim of the skull). This suggests that the flow of the cerebrospinal fluid has been blocked and the back pressure has caused the ventricles to expand greatly. This is the appearance of normal pressure hydrocephalus and the symptoms could be helped by the insertion of a shunt to relieve the pressure.

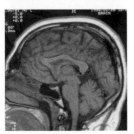

Figure 2.7 This is a picture of a magnetic resonance imaging scan of the brain taken from the side. The grey line going down to the bottom of the picture is the spinal cord and above that is the brainstem. To the right of that, the tree–like structure is the cerebellum. The cerebral cortex is the large grey area occupying most of the inside of the head. The person is looking to the left.

Another type of scan that is sometimes carried out is called a SPET (single photon emission tomography) scan. In this, a radioisotope is injected into a vein in the arm and a camera (similar to that used in a CT scan) can give an accurate picture of the level of blood flow to various parts of the brain. This can be particularly useful in the diagnosis of dementia of the frontal lobe type. Another type of brain scan, which is not yet used in clinical practice but which you may have heard about, is called PET (position emission tomography) which shows the metabolism of the brain.

Very occasionally, it is necessary to do a lumbar puncture to examine the cerebrospinal fluid. This involves a person lying on their side in a bed and having a needle inserted in the base of their spine to draw off some fluid. This is a very safe and routine procedure, although the person usually needs to stay in hospital during the day for this to be carried out.

When a doctor or nurse has all this information available, a 'formulation' is made of an individual case and a diagnosis and treatment plan can be offered.

Summary
Examination of a person with suspected dementia
- Mental state examination
  Depression
  Memory and associated features
- Physical examination
  Check for signs of a stroke
  Check for risk factors for a stroke
- Detailed tests of memory (neuropsychological tests)
- Investigations
  Blood tests
  Brain scan
  Chest x-ray
  Electrocardiogram
  Electroencephalogram
  Lumbar puncture

3 THE MANAGEMENT OF DEMENTIA

The impact of dementia

The experience of dementia is frequently described as a journey. The person with dementia begins this journey alone with the personal recognition that there is a change in their abilities or memory performance. As the changes progress, others join the person with dementia on their journey to offer support or companionship. Some companions on the journey travel only a short distance, perhaps offering specific services at specific times, whilst others go the full distance. This section is about this journey and the impact that dementia can have upon those who are challenged to undertake it.

The impact of memory impairment on the person with dementia

Whatever the severity of the symptoms of dementia, they will always have an impact upon the person who experiences them and this impact will usually be evident to others because of changes in the mood or behaviour of the person with dementia.

The symptoms of dementia have been described earlier in this book and we can summarise them as being:

* *amnesia* – loss of memory
* *aphasia* – difficulty with language
* *apraxia* – an inability to carry out physical tasks (such as using a knife and fork)
* *agnosia* – an inability to recognise people and objects
* *associated features* – psychiatric symptoms and behaviour disturbances.

All these symptoms are being brought about by the illness or disability that the person with dementia is experiencing. However, in the case of the associated features, which may include changes in mood or behaviour such as agitation or depression, it is possible that they may also occur as a direct consequence of the way in which the person with dementia feels about themselves or reacts to the care that others may offer. It is these specific changes that we will discuss in this section.

Mild dementia

In the early stages of dementia, the person will experience mild and often subtle changes on a day-by-day basis. These changes will always represent a change to that person's previous way of performing and will therefore always be evident to that person. At first they may be so mild as to generate amusement rather than concern and even as they progress the sufferer and others may attempt to disregard them as being the result of age, stress or a busy lifestyle.

This initial stage is often referred to as the 'hidden phase' of a dementing illness, as the changes represent difficulties rather than problems and these difficulties either may not be obvious to others or easily dismissed. However, as they progress, a little further amusement or indifference begins to give way to concern and the person with dementia, or a concerned relative may seek advice from the family doctor.

During the hidden phase of dementia, even mild and subtle changes in performance will have a psychological impact upon the person who experiences them. The impact at this early stage could be considered as consisting of anxiety and frustration, the combination of which results in behaviour changes.

The person with developing dementia is aware of the changing nature of their intellectual performance and may begin to become anxious. This anxiety will be expressed through the person's behaviour. They may complain more of mild physical problems such as indigestion or headaches; they may lose concentration easily and become less efficient at work or home; they may start to withdraw from certain activities which are becoming challenging and this may include social activities, so it appears that the person is becoming withdrawn or disinterested. Alongside this worry about their abilities or performance, the person may also become frustrated with themselves when they are unable to remember something or unable to do something which used to be so easy.

This frustration will lead to impatience and irritability and will also result in outbursts of anger usually directed at inanimate objects or at themselves and then at the person closest to them, husband or wife, for example, who may also be verbally abused or blamed for what is happening. These two symptoms of anxiety and frustration are interconnected and exacerbate each other, bringing about a vicious circle in that the more frustrated the person gets the harder it becomes to remember something; the harder it is to remember something, the more anxious they become; the more anxious they become, the harder it is to remember something, and the cycle continues.

An outcome of this cyclical process, and the reinforcement of failure it may bring about, may well be for the person with dementia to become depressed. During the hidden phase of dementia, the onset of memory problems may be dismissed as being the consequence of depression, and certainly there are some similarities between the symptoms of both with apathy, social withdrawal and loss of interest being commonly witnessed. In the later stages of dementia, signs of depression are frequently regarded as being the exacerbation of the dementing illness.

What is often forgotten is that dementia and depression are not mutually exclusive and can frequently coexist. Failure to recognise the symptoms of dementia and dismiss them as depression acts to prolong the hidden phase and failure to recognise depressive symptoms following a diagnosis of dementia serves to deny that person effective treatment.

At this point, with increasing severity of symptoms, we now start to enter the so-called 'apparent phase' of dementia. This is the period of time when others become both aware of and concerned by the presence of memory problems in the person with dementia and the changes in mood and behaviour that they are causing. Very often there are common experiences which occur and propel us forward into the apparent phase. These include:

- getting lost when driving in a familiar place or frequently losing the car;
- becoming very repetitive in conversation or making frequent and repetitive phone calls to family members;
- getting dressed and leaving for work when that person has been retired for a number of years;
- causing domestic fires by forgetting to turn off the cooker or other appliances;
- becoming disoriented to time and standing outside shops or other places during the night or early hours of the morning;
- having very little recall of significant current events involving the family and angry when asked about them;
- becoming unable to use familiar household appliances such as kettle or electric razor and becoming frustrated and impatient when attempting to use them.

Even though the person is now entering a new phase of the dementing illness and even though problems are becoming apparent to others, it does not necessarily follow that a diagnosis of dementia will now be made. Sometimes the changes from a clinical perspective may be so mild as not to raise a suspicion of dementia and the family doctor does not feel that referral to a specialist service is required. Eventually, however, the dementing illness progresses and the frequency and severity of symptoms increases to the point where it is readily apparent to all that a problem exists.

Moderate dementia
For most of this period the person with dementia will be experiencing moderate to moderately severe symptoms of their illness. At this stage the person is no longer just having memory lapses, but these have become real problems and are making a significant impact upon their everyday life. Common problems, which would suggest moderate dementia, could include:

- no longer recalling your address;
- getting lost frequently in very familiar places including own home;
- no longer recognising familiar objects such as a telephone;
- beginning to lose the understanding of others' speech;
- beginning to have difficulty talking;
- inability to make decisions or solve problems;
- becoming dependent upon others for cooking or shopping.

These problems clearly suggest that the person with dementia is becoming more disabled by their particular illness and again this deterioration can be witnessed through changes in their mood and behaviour.

Some of the most evident changes will reflect the growing detachment from reality that the person with dementia is experiencing. This sense of disorientation is itself a progressive phenomenon, causing that person to become increasingly uncertain, unsure and perplexed by everyday life. The classic presentation of disorientation is for it to occur in a cumulative fashion and the extent of the uncertainty is suggestive of the severity of that person's dementia. The commonly experienced disorientations in descending order are:

- date
- day of the week
- month
- year
- season
- place
- others' identities
- personal identity.

The experience of becoming progressively disoriented or detached from reality is frequently termed 'confusion', but such a bland term does little to convey the often frightening nature of becoming suspended in a reality that is no longer familiar or which cannot be understood. By the stage of moderate dementia, the level of disorientation will have moved on from affecting time relationships to now affecting relationship to place and awareness of the identities of others. Not surprisingly, a state in which the person is markedly distanced from our understanding of reality will have a significant impact upon their mood and behaviour.

Feeling uncertain around other people or in unfamiliar environments may make that person reluctant to be away from home where they will feel safer and more in control. This may be perceived as that person becoming less sociable or less motivated to do new things or to visit new places. This social reluctance will be worsened if that person retains an insight into their problems with memory and possibly speech, as they will experience embarrassment or feel challenged by the expectations of social activity.

The focus of everyday life therefore starts to become reduced as facets of that everyday life become challenging and anxiety provoking. Life may now appear to revolve almost exclusively around the needs of the person with dementia. It will seem that they have become selfish or indifferent to the needs of others. In reality the disabilities brought about by dementia are so dominant that the person experiencing them will find attempts at comprehending or appreciating others' needs as much a challenge as trying to understand life in general. Mental resources will be diminished and taking up these challenges exhausting; consequently the person's attention and energy is devoted to making sense of life.

Acting to further confound this situation are the other facets of dementia and in particular difficulties with communication. A number of speech and language symptoms may occur and these include:

- word-finding problems
- naming difficulties
- use of inappropriate words
- repetition
- misunderstanding of others' speech.

Being suspended in a reality different from our own, which is possibly frightening, certainly perplexing, and not being able to verbally communicate this bewilderment serves to further isolate the person with dementia. Alternative means of communication may well develop to articulate these feelings of distress or needs which are not being met. Commonly, behaviour may be the method of communication. Often this behaviour is termed problematic and may include:

- aggression
- shouting or screaming
- crying
- wandering
- agitation
- restlessness.

They may be better described as challenging behaviours because we are being challenged to understand the message that is being conveyed.

Some people with dementia may become aggressive to others and this may be an attempt to communicate fear, anxiety, uncertainty or pain. Some may shout or scream as a response to under-stimulation, to boredom or frustration. Crying may indicate depression and wandering may suggest that memories of previously purposeful activity have resurfaced or that the person is trying to find something or distance themselves from negative feelings by trying to walk away from them.

A significant change in the person with moderate dementia and expressed through their behaviour is the changing nature of that person's ability to function in day-to-day activities. Dementia robs people of their ability to function in their normal everyday manner. This is again progressive and as functioning becomes impaired others need to assist and to assume a greater degree of responsibility.

For the person with dementia who retains some insight, this dependency upon others will further induce feelings of distress, frustration, worthlessness and anger. Where insight has been lost, the person with dementia may angrily reject or resist the essential care of others.

Severe dementia

The nature of dementia is for problems with memory and functioning to progress to the point at which that person becomes very significantly disabled and very highly dependent upon others. The final severest and terminal stage of all dementias occurs at the very end of the illness that has brought about the dementia and represents the very end of what may have been an arduous journey.

In this stage, the person with dementia will appear to be very changed from when they developed mild difficulties and commenced the journey. Common symptoms will now include:

- no noticeable memory ability
- no functional ability
- a high level of dependency upon others
- incontinence
- no effective communication ability
- sporadic episodic challenging behaviours.

The person with severe dementia is now markedly affected by their illness and will eventually die as even the basic ability of the body to fight infections or to regulate normal functioning is now affected. This can be a traumatic stage of the illness for the carer, particularly as it is difficult to understand what the person with dementia is experiencing and the realisation that the companion on that long journey no longer shares any recognition or remembrance of the experience.

The time a person is in each of the three stages varies enormously. Dementia can last anything between 2 and 20 years, the average after diagnosis being about 5–7 years (although it can vary at what stage a person receives diagnosis). As a very rough guide, about 50% of the illness is spent in the mild stage, and about 25% in each of the moderate and severe stages.

The impact of memory impairments on others
Dementia, therefore, very clearly has a definite impact upon the person affected by it but also, very clearly, they are not the only ones to experience its impact. Others who have a relationship with the sufferer may often be as affected in terms of their emotions and behaviour. Usually these other people will have a significant relationship with the sufferer such as close family member or friend, but they may also have a less significant relationship such as a work colleague or occasional acquaintance. The degree to which these other people are affected by the sufferer's difficulties depends upon three closely related factors:
- the nature of the relationship;
- the severity of the sufferer's difficulties;
- the way in which the sufferer responds to their difficulties.

The closer that you are to a person experiencing memory impairments, the more you will feel their impact upon you and your life. In terms of relationships, we are talking about any of the following:
- spouse or partner
- dependant or adult offspring
- parent
- sibling

- friend
- work colleague or employee
- social acquaintance
- neighbour

Although we would traditionally regard the first few on the list as being examples of important relationships, it is important to recognise that in reality any of the above can, depending on individual circumstances, constitute a significant relationship.

In general terms, a significant relationship would imply that some part of everyday life involves the sufferer and that a strong emotional bond exists between both people. In many couples, there will be a mutual responsibility for decision making, problem solving or planning, alongside a relationship built upon affection, trust and understanding, and to a lesser extent other significant relationships are built upon the same foundations.

Memory impairment of whatever severity acts to erode these foundations and to make those relationships fragile and vulnerable to change for the worse. In the case of a progressive illness, such as Alzheimer's disease, it may be that part of the progression is for some relationships to end, some to change and some to become more difficult, in much the same way as companions on the journey into dementia come and go.

As memory performance declines then, everyday life becomes disrupted. In mild dementia, such disruption may be fairly minimal whilst in moderate or severe impairment it may be catastrophic. A large part of this disruption occurs because of the fact that whatever the relationship, there will always be a greater responsibility placed upon the person who does not have a memory impairment. In memory impairments that persist or progress then, this devolving of responsibility will occur more and more, leading to a distinct inequality in the relationship. Shared activities will cease to be shared and the non-sufferer will be forced to assume a more dominant role, which may itself represent a significant change in that relationship.

In mild memory loss, the carer may need to remind the sufferer about appointments, may need to leave written notes, or may need to start taking sole responsibility for important things such as paying bills. As the impairments progress and become more severe, the carer may have to assume almost total responsibility for household management, for driving or organising transport, and may even need to remind the sufferer about personal care such as having a bath or wearing clean clothes.

Alongside the severity of the impairment, it is also important to remember the toll these problems levy on the sufferer because how they react to them will often dictate how the non-sufferer reacts and what changes occur within the relationship. The impact on the sufferer has been discussed previously but for the purposes of this section we can consider their reaction in fairly simplistic terms of positive or negative.

A positive reaction would usually occur in early stages of dementia and could encompass a willingness to seek help or to develop routines that help to minimise the difficulties, and a verbal appreciation to the non-sufferer for the extra work that they may have to do.

A negative approach could occur at any level of severity and would encompass such things as denying that a problem exists, readily blaming others when things are forgotten or becoming angry or abusive. In cases of dementia, we could also include challenging behaviours or psychiatric symptoms, such as hallucinations or delusions, if they occur as negative factors. Having stated this, it is crucial also to say that we should not blame those sufferers who do react in a negative way as often this may well be simply a further symptom over which they have no control.

A positive reaction in the sufferer will also make it easier for the non-sufferer to adopt a positive attitude whilst a negative reaction will worsen the experience for the non-sufferer and will serve to rapidly challenge their own emotional health. The key to responding positively to the experience of dementia is working together as a partnership, being honest, and openly addressing the problems and challenges that arise.

To do so, it is important to understand that the carer will be affected physically and emotionally by the sufferer's impairments and when considering

the commonest ways in which your mood or behaviour may change it is also important to remember that:
- the closer the relationship to the sufferer, the greater will be these changes in mood and behaviour of the carer.
- a negative reaction in the sufferer will increase the severity of the changes in mood and behaviour.

Changes to the carer's mood and behaviour may occur in response to the impairments at any level of severity. There is, however, often a commonly occurring cumulative process, which means that the changes brought about by mild impairments are also brought about by moderate impairments, but extra ones also occur. It may therefore be useful to consider the changes that can happen to the carer at each level of severity.

Table 3.1   Carer's mood and behaviour in response to severity of patient's memory impairment

Patient	Carer
Mild memory impairments	Irritated Frustrated Angry Impatient Argumentative Amused Unloved Under appreciated
Moderate memory impairments	All the above but to a greater extent No longer amused Worried or anxious that a problem exists Assuming greater responsibility Loss of confidence in the sufferer Dislike of the sufferer Tearful or upset Poor concentration Mild memory difficulty Mild depression
Severe memory impairments	All the above but to a greater extent Isolation Exhaustion Physical complaints Stress Guilt

As well as understanding that changes can occur, it is also crucial to remember that carers of people with dementia do cope and do survive the journey they have embarked upon. Studies of carers have demonstrated the positive ways in which they have been able to cope. Some of the common methods have included:

- blaming the illness, not the person affected by it;
- taking life one day at a time;
- trying to see the funny side of things;
- preserving a little bit of time for yourself;
- having an interest outside of caring;
- sharing feelings of anger and resentment openly with others.

All these positive ways of coping seem to share an ability to keep a certain perspective on things, but this is difficult to achieve since the carer is, after all, not a neutral observer. It is very easy to succumb to ways of coping and behaving which carers have described as being unhelpful. Very common reasons are not accepting that there is a problem and trying to deny or ignore its real presence and refusing offers of help from others.

It is important to understand that if the experience of dementia is a journey, then it is one that is going to be difficult and at times exhausting. Along the way there will without doubt come a point of time where the carer can no longer give the level of care that is required. Handing over care for an hour a day, a weekend, or permanently will never be easy and carers often feel guilty, humiliated, ashamed, or as if they have betrayed that person.

The reality is that the impact of the illness is powerful and often the promise, made in the early days after diagnosis, never to admit the person with dementia into care is one that can rarely be kept. Accepting this, being open about it and mutually planning early on will do something to ameliorate the feelings carers experience.

Very many carers have described the positive impact that dementia brings. Some liken the post-diagnostic feeling to one of comrades in adversity and for many this strengthens the emotional ties underpinning their relationship. Others have described caring as giving them an opportunity to express, in a very practical way, their gratitude for what may have been a long and loving relationship. Some carers have described how responding to the challenging behaviours of dementia, through tact, gentleness and sensitivity, have presented an opportunity to engage in courting that person again with displays of love, attentiveness and attempts to make that person happy.

Finally, it would appear that making a positive adjustment to the experience of dementia rests upon the following:

- knowing and understanding the diagnosis;
- openly sharing problems and concerns;
- mutually planning for the future;
- accepting help when it is offered.

Memory-retraining strategies

As we get older, some aspects of our memory will decline as a natural consequence of the ageing process. However, this normal decline differs from a disease process such as Alzheimer's disease in several different ways. Many people report a decline in memory as they get older, and the research does support this view. When an older person is required to take in new information, retain it, organise and store it, often whilst still attending to incoming information, performance can be impaired compared with a younger group of adults. Are these differences due to a superior educational system that benefits young people? Not really, because even when older and younger people are matched for number of years of education, there are still pronounced differences that are attributable to age. However, if guidance is given in terms of helping older people take in the information, and if support is available at recall, these changes can be minimised.

Age-related 'benign' memory loss can affect different types of memory. For example, normal older people may find it difficult to remember where and when an event took place, or may have problems with the recall of items that are unrelated. Particular difficulties occur with the acquisition of new skills and learning in older adults. Skills such as playing a musical instrument, reading or driving usually remain intact. Older people who have well practised skills in certain areas, and who maintain them, can be as efficient as younger people in these areas.

Many studies over the years have reported poor results from efforts to help to improve the memory of people with Alzheimer's disease. It is not really that there is a high degree of failure, as many of the methods used to teach people with Alzheimer's disease have used methods that have been successful in groups of healthy older people. One such method is the use of visual imagery, which is often used with healthy older people. This involves the creation of a 'picture' in the mind's eye that helps memory. For example, if a list of words is to be remembered, then it might be worth putting them together in a 'picture'. Say the words were: cup, hat, bandage, cake and tablet, then a visual image might take the format shown in this illustration.

Thus the ' picture' for these five words could take the form of a woman wearing a hat, carrying a tray with a cup on it, a piece of cake, tablets (indigestion remedy), with her foot all bandaged up (maybe from having dropped a large slab of cake on it). The use of a technique such as this is often very effective at aiding memory in healthy people. However, if the same technique is used to help a person with Alzheimer's disease, they are more likely to fail.

Why should this be? The reason is probably that this type of method is, in actual fact, quite difficult to perform. Even in healthy older people, a good imagination is required in order to put all the items into the picture, and often it needs to be done quickly. Also it depends on the 'picture' being remembered, so the visual memory needs to be performing fairly well. In Alzheimer's disease, the ability to concentrate, to put together a 'picture' quickly, and to remember it can be poor, so this type of memory aid is not likely to be useful. The whole procedure is just too complex.

Summary
- As everyone grows older, memory tends to get worse.
- People with dementia can improve their memory performance.
- They need to be given help specifically tailored to their abilities.
- The type of assistance may differ from traditional teaching methods that are used for teaching healthy older adults.

However, more encouragingly, there are some studies that have shown that people with Alzheimer's disease can, under certain conditions, improve memory performance. Some of these techniques are described below.

Spaced retrieval technique
This is a teaching method that involves the recall of information at short intervals initially, with a gradual increase in the time interval. For example, if the task was to be learning that the day of the week is Friday, the person would be asked maybe every 3 minutes, 'what day of the week is it today?' As gradual improvement is made, the time interval is increased from 3 to 5 minutes. If, however, they fail to get the answer right at 5 minutes, the whole procedure reverts back to the 3-minute interval, or whatever the time span was that enabled them to get the correct answer. If this does not lead to improvement, then the interval is halved. Accurate recall after a 5–10 minute interval is deemed to be success according to the researchers who recommend this technique. The advantages of the 'spaced retrieval' technique is that it requires little effort from the person with Alzheimer's disease, and there is some evidence that often the learning becomes almost automatic and people can give the right answer without having to think about it. Also, probably because there is a high rate of success, people enjoy this method of training. Carers can be taught the basic principles of spaced retrieval and can incorporate it into their daily routines. People with mild and moderate Alzheimer's disease have been able to learn and recall information such as:
- faces and names;
- where certain objects have been placed;
- the names of objects;
- items such as day of the week, month, and date, etc.

Summary
- Spaced retrieval technique is a teaching method that involves the recall of information at short intervals initially, with a gradual increase in the time span.

Method of vanishing cues

This is a method that attempts to improve verbal memory skills by giving letters as clues as to the required word. For example, if we wanted to teach the name JANE, we might give the first three letters in the name: J A N _ If the person is unable to produce the name, letters are progressively added until the correct name is attained. On the next training session one letter will be taken away. For example, J A _ _ and so on until the learning progresses. If a person fails at any point, then letters are added to help them. This technique has been used with success in teaching people to learn names and occupations of staff members, also addresses, telephone numbers and recognition of objects. In many cases the learning has been maintained for several weeks.

Summary
- The method of vanishing cues attempts to improve verbal memory skills by giving letters/numbers as clues to the required answer.

Errorless learning

This technique has been around for many years, but has only recently been used with people with Alzheimer's disease. In the main it has been helpful for teaching people with learning disabilities and people who have had a head injury, or brain disease of some kind. When people with Alzheimer's disease learn new information, they are often prone to failure. Let's take an example of a typical learning scenario, such as learning a list of pairs using a traditional approach:
- fruit – apple
- metal – iron
- baby – cries

After having read out the list of pairs, the psychologist would say: 'which word goes with fruit?' If the person with Alzheimer's disease does not know the answer, it is very tempting to encourage them to guess, 'it's worth a try'. The problem with this is they probably know the answer is a fruit and a guess might yield the wrong answer, so instead of 'fruit – apple', they may guess 'fruit – banana', which is obviously wrong, although a sensible guess. This wrong answer, however, then is almost locked in to the brain and the person finds it difficult to correct it. Consequently, the next time he is asked 'what word went with fruit', he will inevitably reply 'banana'.

This is what we call errorful learning. Errorless learning is a method that prevents errors being made during training. It differs from errorful learning primarily because guessing is not encouraged. If a person does not know the right answer, they are given the answer, and therefore prevented from making errors. In the preliminary studies that have used this method there have been some good results. One study found that four participants were able to relearn face-name pairs, and recall personal information. In some of the cases the information had been retained over a period of 6 months.

Summary
- Errorless learning is a technique that prevents errors from being made during training.

Sensorimotor skills

Several researches have found that the ability to perform certain simple skills are preserved in Alzheimer's disease. These might include tasks that have a 'motor' element to them; this usually means that they are tasks that involve a degree of manual dexterity, albeit at fairly simple level. Such tasks might be: combing hair, washing, brushing teeth, preparation and eating meals, etc. The training would involve written and/or verbal instructions, and the task might be broken down into smaller goals so that each stage of the 'action' is taught before it is put together as a whole. Thus the task is simplified and built up gradually.

Similarly, motor skills that people have built up over a lifetime can often be maintained at some level, even in the moderate stage of the illness. Activities such as painting, musical instrument playing, etc., can be stimulated with good results. Interestingly, it has been found that there may also be 'knock-on' effects of this type of training, in that often 'untrained' skills also improve spontaneously. It is almost as if stimulation and encouragement of certain motor activities improves other practical skills.

It seems to be successful due to the fact that certain parts of the brain have been relatively spared from the disease process. Many of the benefits seen are quite extensive, and can be maintained for a considerable period of time. The gloomy predictions of the past that people with Alzheimer's disease are not capable of learning information are now becoming outdated, and we should be moving towards an era where we are able to help individuals fulfil their potential despite the ravages of this disease.

Summary
- Simple, well practised tasks that usually involve a degree of manual dexterity can often be encouraged and maintained with good results.

General techniques
These tend to be used when people develop moderate to severe Alzheimer's disease and before the recent advances in drugs were considered to be the main treatment methods for improving memory.

Reality orientation
This can take two forms:
- classroom based, and
- 24-hour reality orientation and attempts to improve orientation and personal information.

Classroom based orientation takes place in a group situation, is of a fixed duration and is usually led by an Occupational Therapist. Demands on the group are minimal, as questions and comments are raised concerning the following areas:
- weather
- day, month, date
- history, etc.

As the name suggests, 24-hour reality orientation is meant to be ongoing. It involves the continued repetition of information (again focusing on weather, day, date, time, etc.) by staff, or anyone who is interacting with the person.

In effect, reality orientation is a procedure whereby certain topics are constantly being brought up and practised. There is some evidence that it can help with aspects of memory and thinking and behaviour, but that it has little benefits for the completion of practical tasks required for everyday life.

Reminiscence therapy
This focuses on the production of historical information that may stimulate long-term memories for the person with Alzheimer's disease. For example, photographs of a monarch's coronation, famous politicians, or wartime scenes may evoke discussion and further memories. There is not a great deal of scientific evidence to support this therapy, although there are some doctors who say it is beneficial. In essence, this type of therapy is probably working because it is tapping into long-term memory skills, which are usually better preserved than short-term memory. This has implications for carers wanting to apply this type of therapy at home. Compiling a scrapbook with photographs, letters, etc., can form a 'personalised' reminiscence book, focusing on interests, family, or aspects of work that have been important to the person during his life. When communication abilities are lost, this type of tool can often help carers and relatives to interact, albeit at a reduced level.

External aids

Non-electronic
External memory aids such as diaries, calendars, signs and wipe-clean boards are useful aids for memory. In one study a 'memory book' was produced which contained pictures of daily activities in conjunction with a clock face showing the right time for them to be carried out.

Electronic
As electronic devices become more advanced, it seems appropriate to look at their usefulness for people with Alzheimer's disease. They can take over the role of prompting and reminding from the carer. For example, at a certain predetermined time, an alarm could go off followed by a verbal message.

Summary
- Memory aids such as diaries, calendars, signs and wipe-clean boards can be easily produced and effective.
- There is some evidence that electronic devices can be helpful.

Treatment of dementia

When considering the treatment of dementia, one can talk about non-drug treatment, such as behaviour therapy and psychological support, and drug treatment. Each of these can be applied to two of the expressions of dementia:
- psychiatric symptoms and behavioural disturbances; and
- memory loss and other neuropsychological features.

Non-drug treatment of psychiatric symptoms and behavioural disturbances

Many of the psychiatric symptoms and, later in the disease, the behavioural disturbances of dementia, can be managed and treated very effectively without the need for drugs. The first thing that a doctor or nurse would do would be to make sure that the patient and carer understood that the symptoms, generally speaking, arise as a consequence of the disease. For example, if a person suffering from dementia misplaces a wallet or handbag, they may accuse someone else of moving it, or even having stolen it. A brief explanation that this can be seen as a natural response to forgetting where something is can be helpful. A strategy such as always putting a wallet or handbag or set of keys in one place can be helpful.

If someone has an idea that is firmly held, there is little point in trying to convince them that they are wrong. For example, some people with dementia say that their parents are still alive when the fact is that they are dead. Sometimes a carer will try and get the person with dementia to say what age they are and then to calculate what age their parents would be if alive, in order to prove they are wrong. This is an unhelpful approach and could be seen as serving only to humiliate the person with dementia. On the other hand, it is important not to agree with somebody with an erroneous idea, especially if that idea is clearly abnormal. The secret is probably never to completely agree or disagree but somehow take the middle ground.

It is very common for people with dementia to repeat the same question again and again. It is best for the carer to avoid becoming irritable with the person and accept that they simply cannot remember. A technique, which may be helpful in this situation, is validation therapy.

Validation therapy is a technique that suggests that in many instances reorientation is not always the most appropriate or correct approach. Instead, the validation therapy approach involves working with the emotional content of what is being said rather than the actual words being used.

Repeatedly asking 'where is mother?', for example, suggests to us verbally that the person asking the question is not oriented to our reality but is clearly recalling a previous time when mother was a significant part of life. In this situation, reality orientation would serve to remind the person of that, often quite harshly, but would not address the feelings or emotions that are being expressed behind the question.

On the other hand, validation therapy focuses upon these feelings, which will be very real to the person with dementia. They may be anxious or worried about mother who in their reality should be present and this may lead to distress or agitation. In other situations, people may have feelings of anger, sadness, frustration, despondency or despair, which lie behind apparently disoriented comments or questions.

Effective communication in validation therapy terms is based upon accepting these feelings as being very real, taking them seriously and responding to them in a way which shows we understand and are prepared to share that person's feelings. This may involve simply sitting with that person, talking about the way they are feeling, offering reassurance, smiles and gentleness until the distress begins to fade away.

The principle behind this is to accept that recurrent themes emerge in repetitive questions or repetitive speech and that these themes reflect unmet needs or anxieties on the part of the person with dementia. Often old memories of significant life experiences can emerge and dominate that person's reality for a period of time. Validation therapy gives us a way of entering into and sharing that person's reality to offer support and reassurance. The person who asks repeatedly 'where is mother?' may be reliving significant memories of mother. Rather than reminding them that mother has been dead for some years, which is a harsh approach, the carer can talk with them about mother but always using the past tense. An opening comment such as: 'You're clearly thinking about your mother; she must have been a very important person in your life. Tell me what she was like' allows the person with dementia to express their concerns and anxieties, to talk about their mother and often to gradually remind themselves that mother passed away some time ago.

Some behaviours, such as aggression or screaming in the later stages of dementia, can be treated with what are called behavioural techniques. It is important to reinforce good behaviour and avoid constant reprimands for bad behaviour. When someone with dementia becomes agitated or excited, it is important to try and step back from the situation and to identify anything that seems to cause a particular behaviour, anything that seems to keep it happening, and anything that seems to stop the behaviour. It may be that patterns will emerge which would be helpful in understanding and managing a particular symptom. For example, it is not uncommon for people with dementia to become agitated and excited in the evening. It may become apparent that a woman suffering from dementia is expecting her husband home for his dinner and because he has not appeared, she is getting worried and agitated about where he is.

Understanding the behaviour of the person with dementia rests almost exclusively upon trying to understand more about the person who is experiencing dementia. Adopting a person-centred approach reminds us that it is the unique individual who is important rather than the label or diagnosis they have acquired. Everyone with dementia has a unique life history, set of relationships, personality, habits and preferences. Understanding these can often help to determine the context of challenging behaviours and the messages, which lie behind such behaviours.

The most important thing to remember when dealing with psychiatric symptoms or behaviour disturbances and trying to manage them without drugs, is to understand that the person's actions are not under conscious control and it is important to avoid getting angry and frustrated. This is easier said than done! Also, and often contrary to popular belief, people with memory loss are able to respond to a kind, gentle and consistent approach and it is very important to try a strategy like this before resorting to drugs.

There are a number of other treatments that can help control agitation in people with severe dementia. A technique called 'the snoozelen' is a room where there are noises, music, and things to touch and feel. This approach can decrease agitation in people with dementia. Likewise, there is some evidence that light therapy (where someone with dementia sits in front of a light box) can make people feel calmer.

Summary
- Try a non-drug approach to manage behavioural problems first.
- Explanations for the reasons behind behaviours can be very helpful.
- Avoid challenging the person with dementia even if they are obviously wrong.
- The reactions of a person with dementia are not under their own control

Drug treatment of psychiatric symptoms and behavioural disturbances

If symptoms and behaviours are very distressing for the patient, or very distressing and disturbing for a carer, or the non-drug approaches have failed, it may be appropriate to consider a drug treatment. This is something that the general practitioner or a community psychiatric nurse can advise on.

There are several different types of drugs that may be helpful.

Antidepressants

These treat symptoms of depression and can either be used if someone with dementia becomes depressed or if someone has a depressive illness and some symptoms of memory loss. There are a number of antidepressant drugs and in terms of their effect on depression there is probably very little to choose between them. Some of the older drugs tend to have more side-effects (e.g. amitriptyline, which can give a dry mouth, constipation, blurred vision and dizziness), whilst some of the newer ones have fewer side-effects (e.g. sertraline, although this can cause stomach upset). Some antidepressants have a sedative effect, but that can be an advantage if someone with depression is agitated or excited.

Neuroleptics

These are quite powerful drugs and are used to treat schizophrenia in younger people but can be very helpful in controlling aggression, agitation and delusions. Like the antidepressants, there are older and newer types. The older drugs, e.g. chlorpromazine, thioridazine, promazine and haloperidol, tend to have more side-effects and can cause very stiff muscles and some of the symptoms of Parkinson's disease. These side-effects are particularly marked in people with Lewy body dementia. Some of the newer neuroleptics (risperidone or olanzapine) tend to be less sedative and have fewer side-effects. However, if someone is very agitated and upset, it still may be appropriate to prescribe one of the older drugs. Very occasionally in someone with dementia, the drugs can be given by an intramuscular injection. This is particularly useful if it is very difficult for someone to take tablets, but is something that should only be considered by a specialist.

Sedatives

These are drugs that generally make people calmer and can make them sleep. Examples are benzodiazepines (such as lorazepam, nitrazepam, temazepam and diazepam), clomethiazole, and a number of sleeping agents (such as zopiclone). If there is no evidence of delusions, but the patient is just slightly agitated, these drugs can be very effective. A drug called sodium valproate (which has been used in epilepsy) can also be useful in controlling agitation.

Drugs are generally available in a number of different forms such as a liquid, capsule or tablet and it is usually possible to find a formulation that suits an individual.

Summary
- Effective drugs are available to treat behavioural problems.
- Antidepressants can be effective.
- Sedatives can be effective.
- Newer drugs can have fewer side-effects than older ones.
  However, a drug that works is better than one that doesn't!

Non-drug treatment of memory loss and other neuropsychological features are described fully earlier in this chapter.

Drug treatment of memory loss and other neuropsychological features
This area has generated the most interest, and many drug companies are trying to develop medicines for the prevention and treatment of dementia, especially that caused by Alzheimer's disease.

Anticholinesterase drugs
These are commonly known as anti-dementia drugs. They work in the following way. The destruction of the brain by deposits of the abnormal protein results in a chemical deficiency of a brain chemical (neurotransmitter) called acetylcholine. Acetylcholine is made in the nerve cells and is used by these cells to communicate with each other. There is an enzyme that breaks down acetylcholine, which is called cholinesterase. If this enzyme is blocked, less of the acetylcholine is broken down and the net effect therefore is to get a raised level of the neurotransmitter (Figure 3.1). Research has shown that in patients with Alzheimer's disease there is real improvement when people are given these drugs. Because they act against the enzyme that breaks down acetylcholine, they are called anticholinesterase drugs.

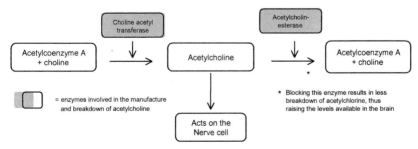

Figure 3.1 Acetylcholine in the brain.

The first drug that was available was called tacrine. Although this produced significant benefit to people, its use was limited because in some people it damaged their liver. Three drugs of this type are now available (drugs usually have two names, a chemical name which describes the structure of the drug and a trade name which is the name the drug company gives it when sold). Donepezil (trade name Aricept) was the first to be licensed in the UK. The next was rivastigmine (trade name Exelon), which was followed by galantamine (trade name Reminyl) which comes from daffodils. These drugs have all been shown to be effective in improving objective tests of memory in people with mild to moderate Alzheimer's disease and also in improving global measures of well-being. (Global measures of well-being is an index, overall, of whether a patient is better on a particular drug and takes into account all the symptoms that a patient has and also includes the view of the carers). In the experience of the authors the side-effects of the drugs are minimal, dizziness and stomach upsets being the most common. There is evidence that the improvement can last for up to 12 months or perhaps even longer. There is also evidence that the sooner the drugs are started the better. Whilst the drugs are currently only licensed for the treatment of mild to moderate Alzheimer's disease, some studies are underway looking at their effects in more severe illness.

Oestrogens
These are given as part of hormone replacement therapy to women. There is some evidence that taking oestrogen is protective against the development of Alzheimer's disease and some research has suggested that it may actually improve symptoms in people known to have the disorder.

Hydergine
This drug improves blood circulation. Some people who are apathetic and withdrawn and have signs of Parkinson's disease sometimes benefit from the drug, which has an alerting effect.

Aspirin and other anti-inflammatory drugs
There is some evidence that taking indomethacin is protective against the development of Alzheimer's disease and some studies have suggested that aspirin can prevent a second stroke in people who have already had one. A doctor should be consulted before taking aspirin as it can cause stomach ulceration in some people.

Gingko biloba
Some studies have suggested that gingko biloba can improve memory and concentration, but others have produced negative results. Some people describe improvements while taking gingko biloba, but there is not enough evidence to recommend its use.

Antioxidants
Vitamin E may delay the progression of Alzheimer's disease and some people take it for its protective action. It removes substances called free radicals, which can cause nerve cell damage. This is similar to the effect of red wine which in moderation may also be protective against the development of Alzheimer's disease.

Memantine
Mementine (trade name Ebixa) has recently been licensed in the UK for the treatment of moderately severe to severe Alzheimer's disease. It works in a different way to the other agents because it blocks the effect of glutamate, and another brain neurotransmitter which actually has a higher level in Alzheimer's disease. and there is some evidence that these high levels are toxic to brain cells. It helps to stop the toxic effect of glutamate on one of the receptors on the nerve cell (called the NMDA receptor) but it sticks to this receptor relatively weakly - hence its full name, a partial NMDA antagonist. Studies have been carried out in people with more severe Alzheimer's disease (some in nursing homes) which show that the drug could improve symptoms. There is some emerging evidence that combining memantine with the anticholinesterase donepezil can result in additional benefit but further research is needed to confirm, or otherwise, this finding.

Summary
- Drugs are available which can help reverse the memory problems in early Alzheimer's disease.
- Drugs are not a cure.
- Drugs are not effective in everyone.
- Vitamin E, in large doses, can be helpful in slowing the progression of Alzheimer's disease.
- Aspirin can be helpful in preventing strokes.
- Oestrogen may help to prevent Alzheimer's disease.
- There is no scientific evidence that gingko biloba is effective against dementia.
- A doctor should always be consulted before taking anything you can buy without a prescription.

Drugs used to treat dementia

Chemical name	Trade name	Used mainly for
Antidepressants		
Amitriptyline	Lentizol®	Depression
Clomipramine	Anafranil®	Depression
Dothiepin	Prothiaden®	Depression
Imipramine	Tofranil®	Depression
Lofepramine	Gamanil®	Depression
Trazodone	Molipaxin®	Depression/agitation
Moclobemide	Manerix®	Depression
Citalopram	Cipramil®	Depression
Fluoxetine	Prozac®	Depression
Fluvoxamine	Faverin®	Depression
Paroxetine	Seroxat®	Depression
Sertraline	Lustral®	Depression
Mirtazapine	Zispin®	Depression
Nefazodone	Dutonin®	Depression
Venlafaxine	Efexor®	Depression
Neuroleptics		
Chlorpromazine	Largactil®	Aggression/agitation/psychosis
Haloperidol	Haldol®, Serenace®, Dozic®	Aggression/agitation/psychosis
Promazine	Sparine®	Aggression/agitation/psychosis
Thioridazine	Melleril®	Aggression/agitation/psychosis
Trifluoperazine	Stelazine®	Psychosis
Olanzapine	Zyprexa®	Psychosis/agitation
Risperidone	Risperdal®	Psychosis/agitation
Quetiapine	Seroquel®	Psychosis/agitation
Sedatives		
Nitrazepam	Mogadon®	Sedation
Temazepam	Temazepam®	Sleeplessness
Lorazepam	Ativan®	Sedation
Diazepam	Valium®, Valclair®	Sedation
Zolpidem	Stilnoct®	Sleeplessness
Zopiclone	Zimovane®	Sleeplessness
Chloral hydrate	Welldorm®	Sleeplessness
Clomethiazole	Heminevrin®	Agitation
Sodium valproate	Epilim®	Agitation
Anticholinesterase drugs		
Donepezil	Aricept®	To improve memory. (Can also
Rivastigmine	Exelon®	improve psychiatric symptoms
Galantamine	Reminyl®	and behavioural disturbance.)

4 WHAT SHOULD YOU DO IF YOU THINK YOU HAVE A MEMORY PROBLEM?

If you have noticed a change in your memory there are a few important things to think about and consider.

How long has it been going on?

Any problem with memory needs to be interpreted in the light of its duration. We all forget things from time to time and one or two isolated examples spread over a couple of weeks are probably of little or no significance. Also, you might be someone who has had a memory problem all your life and something that has been going on for 30 or 40 years and has not changed is unlikely to be important. It is just a part of you that you need to learn to live with. Most people with Alzheimer's disease describe an onset of memory loss that goes on over a few months. Any memory problem which has been around for, say, 6 or 9 months and which is getting worse, should be investigated further.

What is your general health like?

It is important to consider what your general health is like. It is very common to develop a poor memory if you are physically unwell, especially with a serious disease. Such people can suffer from episodes of confusion that are short-lived periods of disorientation and memory loss and which usually disappear when the underlying physical illness is treated. Any severe and disabling illness can give rise to memory loss, although it is important that if your memory loss is severe and deteriorating that you do not just to put it down to the effects of the illness without further consideration.

Is there someone else in the family with a memory problem?

There is some evidence that dementia runs in families. There are two main ways in which this can occur. First, there are a few families where the disease is passed from generation to generation. In this situation, the disease is similar to other inherited characteristics, such as blue eyes or blonde hair. There are a few families in the world where large family trees have been built up and the dementia is clearly passed from generation to generation in this way. In this situation, the disease usually comes on when people are in their forties and fifties and tends to be a rather severe form of illness. In general, these families account for only about 2% of all cases of Alzheimer's disease. In some situations, it is possible to have a blood test to determine whether you carry the gene to develop Alzheimer's disease.

The second, and by far the commonest way in which the disease affects families is that it tends to occur more commonly when there is another family member affected. This is an observation that can only be made when a large number of people have been studied. Unlike the situation above, it is not possible to be certain that a particular individual is going to develop Alzheimer's disease. It is analogous to the situation where heart disease, cancer and stroke tend to run in families. There is no blood test in this situation which will be able to tell you whether you will develop Alzheimer's disease. These issues are dealt with in more detail in Chapter 5.

In practice, one of the more important effects of having a family member who suffers from memory problems or dementia is that it is likely that you will come and seek help and treatment far sooner than if there was no family member affected. This is probably because having an affected member of the family will make a person much more aware of the significance and the implication of memory problems and that is a strong stimulus to seek advice and treatment at an early stage.

Am I under stress?

It is common, at times of stress, to forget one or two things. This is basically because you either have too much on your mind or there are a few things on your mind but you are tending to think about them a lot more than usual. It is important to recognise that stress can cause a variety of symptoms including a temporary loss of memory. Generally, if the memory problem has only been around for a short time, if you can clearly link it to stressful events, if it tends to vary from day to day, if it tends to get worse when you are under particular stress, or if it gets better when you are not under stress, then your memory problem is less sinister and worrisome than it might have been. If at all possible, try and cut down on your stress levels. It may be that by becoming aware that stress can cause memory problems, you might worry less about memory loss and improve in that way!

Do I feel depressed?

It is very common for people suffering from depression to complain of memory problems. However, depression is very much more common in people who have dementia than in the normal population. If you have had a previous episode of depression, whether it has been treated by a general practitioner or a specialist, or if you are prone to depression, you should be aware that these symptoms may at least be a contribution to your loss of memory. Some symptoms of depression include:

- fatigue and tiredness;
- subjective feelings of the blues;
- low mood or depression;
- poor appetite;

- sleep disturbance (particularly waking early in the morning);
- weight loss (or more rarely, weight gain);
- loss of enjoyment;
- not looking forward to things;
- not enjoying grandchildren;
- poor concentration;
- irritability (often noticed by others);
- feeling worse in the morning;
- feelings of guilt;
- feeling you have let people down.

If, after having considered all these things, you are still worried about your memory problem, you must go and see your general practitioner. Be prepared to give him or her as much information as you can about your current symptoms and your past history. Be prepared to have a brief test of your memory in the surgery. It is quite in order to take a friend or relative with you – it is always helpful to have someone else there in case there are things the doctor says which you later forget. If you have any questions, then write them down on a piece of paper and take them with you.

5 COMMONLY ASKED QUESTIONS

My father had Alzheimer's disease. Will I get it as well?

In a minority of families, Alzheimer's disease appears to be a genetic condition and is passed from generation to generation in the same way as genetic disorders such as Huntington's chorea or cystic fibrosis. Fortunately, these situations are rare and account for only about 2% of all cases of Alzheimer's disease. In these situations, generally speaking, the condition comes on at a younger age (the person might be in their forties or fifties) and usually it is well known within the family that relatives have died of Alzheimer's disease. In some situations, tragically, half of the people in a family are affected. In these cases, it is likely that the disease results from an abnormality in a single gene. It is possible to have a blood test, which will identify whether a person is a carrier or not of the abnormal gene and that will tell, beyond reasonable doubt, whether that individual will get the disease. It is very important that the test is carried out in conjunction with advice from a skilled genetic counsellor. Not everyone wishes to know whether they will develop a particular disease or not.

However, in the vast majority of cases, there is no simple genetic defect. That is not to say that genes are not important – as many as one-third of patients have a family history of memory loss, but usually it is just one affected member. It is likely in these situations that environmental factors are as much a cause of the disease as genetic factors. In the same way that cancer, heart disease and strokes run in families, so does dementia. This is said to be a genetic tendency to develop the disease.

If you are worried about a genetic risk, try and find out as much as you can from relatives and others who might remember the individual who has had memory problems. It is important to get an estimate of what age the person was when the symptoms started, what exactly the symptoms were, whether they had any other illnesses such as a stroke or a heart attack, and how long they lived before they died. It would be helpful to know if anyone remembers whether or not a doctor or health professional put a name to the condition. Very rarely, a person may have had a post-mortem examination and information may be available from that which would help to identify the condition.

Is there a blood test for Alzheimer's disease?

In those rare situations where the disease is obviously passed from generation to generation, a blood test, as mentioned above, can allow an individual to learn whether they are likely to develop Alzheimer's disease or not. In other cases there is no blood test.

A lot has been said about the blood test to measure a chemical in the blood, apolipoprotein E, which carries cholesterol around the body. Apolipoprotein E exists in three forms, called 2, 3 or 4. As we inherit one gene each from our mother and father, we can have any combination of these, i.e. E2/E2, E3/E3, E4/E4, E2/E3, E2/E4 and E3/E4. People who have one or two of the E4 proteins are at greatly increased risk of developing Alzheimer's disease. The importance of this discovery is that it was able to shed light on the biochemical processes that cause Alzheimer's disease. However, the test is not diagnostic of Alzheimer's disease and is of little help in an individual, because many people have one or two of the E4 protein forms and do not all get Alzheimer's disease, and Alzheimer's disease occurs in the absence of E4.

Can Alzheimer's disease be diagnosed on a brain scan?

There are several types of brain scan. CT or CAT scans and MRI scans can tell you about the structure of the brain. SPET scans or PET scans (see Chapter 2) give details of how the brain works in terms of the way the blood gets to the brain and the way it uses glucose and oxygen. It is like looking into a car engine. CT and MRI is like looking into the engine with it switched off whereas SPET and PET is like looking at the car engine while it is running.

The main reason to carry out a CT scan or an MRI scan is to tell whether there is any damage or abnormalities of the brain that might account for the symptoms. A head injury can cause a bleed in the brain. It can also show whether a person has a brain tumour, either one that arises primarily in the brain (a primary brain tumour) or one that has spread from cancer somewhere else (secondary tumours or metastases). It can also tell whether someone has had a major stroke.

One of the hallmarks of Alzheimer's disease is that there is shrinkage of the brain and this can be demonstrated very well on a CT and on an MRI scan. An MRI scan is a more detailed investigation which does not use any radiation and gives a very detailed outline of the brain. However, it is a more arduous procedure for a patient to go through.

A SPET scan can give valuable evidence of the function of the brain – even if one can see the brain on a CT scan, it may not be working correctly. SPET can provide more detailed information and is very good at showing if there are specific regions of the brain that are not working. At the moment, a PET scan is only used as a research tool.

Another type of investigation is an electroencephalogram (EEG). This actually shows the brain waves. It does this by recording the tiny amounts of electricity that are generated by the brain, and analyses them. It is possible to tell if the overall level of activity of the brain is slowed down and it is very good at diagnosing epilepsy, which may not give rise to classical symptoms such as fits. In certain types of dementia (e.g. Creutzfeldt–Jakob disease) the wave pattern is so specific as to be diagnostic of the condition.

How can I tell if my memory is getting worse?

This is a very subjective thing and there may be instances of things that you can't remember now that you used to remember. That happens to everyone as they get older and someone who is 40 may not be as sharp as they were when they were 20 and someone of 60 may well not be as sharp as they were when they were 40. It is after about the age of 50 that memory loss seems to decline in a significant way. It may be that others have noticed a change and will say to you that they think your memory has deteriorated. A certain amount of worsening is to be expected with increasing age and it is when that deterioration is a lot more than one should expect with age that there is a need to seek advice.

In very rare instances, someone may have had a detailed neuropsychological test of their memory for some reason and if that test is repeated, it can show a decline of the scores over time. It is then possible to estimate whether the decline is of the size that would be expected with normal ageing or whether it indicates something more serious such as the development of dementia.

What symptoms would I have if I was depressed?

The obvious symptoms are low spirits, low mood, having the blues. A number of other symptoms include:

- tiredness and fatigue;
- poor concentration;
- feelings of guilt;
- poor appetite;
- loss of sleep, particularly wakening up early in the morning;
- feeling worse in the morning and tending to get better during the day;
- feelings that life isn't worth living and, in extreme situations, planning to kill oneself;
- loss of enjoyment (e.g. in reading, grandchildren, television); and
- poor memory.

The problem is that depression is a common accompaniment to Alzheimer's disease and some of the symptoms are common between the two disorders. However, there is no evidence to suggest that it is any more difficult to treat the depression which occurs in association with early Alzheimer's disease than it is to treat anyone else with depression. Depressive symptoms should be treated, usually with medication, and that can result in their relief. If you are worried you might be depressed you should go and see your own doctor. Drugs to treat depression nowadays are not addictive and do not worsen memory impairment.

Is it possible to prevent getting dementia?

If one wants to prevent something, it is a great help to know what causes it. The cause of Alzheimer's disease is unknown although there have been a number of theories as to why the disease has been caused. Some of these are things about which you can do nothing. For example, age is associated with an increased risk of dementia but there is nothing you can do about that. As has been mentioned before, there is some evidence that dementia runs in families. Treatments are available for some conditions that are largely genetic in origin (such as diabetes).

There are, however, some things that might help in certain circumstances. Although there is not sufficient evidence at present to be able to recommend any drugs that may have a preventative effect on the development of dementia in general and Alzheimer's disease in particular, there is some evidence that vitamin E and some of the antioxidant vitamins such as vitamin C may have a beneficial effect. There is compelling evidence to suggest that oestrogen may be protective against the development of Alzheimer's disease and whilst this is a real advantage to women taking hormone replacement therapy, there is insufficient evidence to recommend its prescription on its own as a preventive measure. Similarly, there is a strong suggestion that drugs of the non-steroidal anti-inflammatory class, such as indomethacin, can give some protection against the development of Alzheimer's disease. There is a host of herbal remedies, such as gingko biloba, which are said to have positive benefits but have yet to be shown to be of benefit by rigorous scientific study.

There are some things that can potentially be done to reduce the likelihood of vascular dementia, which are the same as those recommended to reduce the likelihood of a stroke. Control of high blood pressure, high cholesterol and diabetes are essential components of such a strategy.

However, it is important to bear in mind that all drugs and medications have side-effects and any individual would be ill advised to take any of these medicines without getting medical advice. For example, oestrogen can increase the incidence of some cancers in women and indomethacin and aspirin can contribute to the formation of stomach ulcers. There is also a suggestion that vitamin E can result in an increased risk of brain haemorrhage, even in low doses.

There was a study some years ago which suggested that smoking was protective against Alzheimer's disease and this caused a lot of publicity. However, more recent evidence has shown this to be a spurious finding and the risks of smoking to general health are so great that it should be avoided. People who drink alcohol to excess, above the safe estimated levels of approximately 28 units a week in men (equivalent to 2 pints of beer every night) and 21 units in women (equivalent to 1.5 glasses of wine every night) is harmful and can cause shrinkage of the brain. However, there is some encouraging evidence that red wine, in particular red Chianti wine, can protect against Alzheimer's disease. It probably does this through the antioxidant effect of some of its components. Of course, it should only be drunk in moderation.

Are my aluminium saucepans dangerous?

Studies on people on renal dialysis showed that those who had high levels of aluminium in their bodies, and in particular their brains, develop a condition very like Alzheimer's disease. There is some evidence that aluminium is

49

deposited in the centre of one of the main changes in the brain of people with Alzheimer's disease (the senile plaque). However, whilst there is no doubt that aluminium in very high doses is toxic to the brain and can cause a clinical syndrome like dementia, it is extremely unlikely that such dangerous consequences could come from ordinary cooking equipment.

Will a good diet prevent me from getting Alzheimer's disease?

There is no evidence that there is any dietary supplement or any dietary advice that can be given which will specifically prevent someone getting dementia. However, a good diet ensures good general health. In addition, people who are overweight are at much more risk of developing a stroke and therefore getting vascular dementia. There is so much evidence that a healthy diet with plenty of fruit and vegetables is good for you that it is something one could generally recommend as being of benefit.

Can stress produce Alzheimer's disease?

Stress is generally a very bad thing and there is increasing evidence that it can affect the hormonal system of the brain and can cause shrinkage. However, it is important to remember that Alzheimer's disease is a physical disease like any other and stress itself could not cause the disorder. Stress can contribute to people having a heart attack, an ulcer and asthma and the risk is probably of the same magnitude in the case of Alzheimer's disease.

What is interesting is that people under stress can often appear more confused and disorientated than normal. For example, to be in a strange environment is often stressful for someone who has a tendency, say, to become confused. A holiday, which even though on the face of it does not seem stressful, can be quite disorientating for an older person and so it may appear that an episode of stress brings out symptoms.

I sometimes forget things. Will my memory get worse?

Everybody forgets something from time to time, particularly if we have a lot on our mind or are under stress. This is a common symptom and does not necessarily mean that you are getting dementia. Symptoms tend to be sinister and worrying and worthy of medical attention if they are so severe that they interfere with your work and social activities on a consistent basis, if others consistently comment on your lack of memory, if you forget things that are very important, if your poor memory does not vary from day to day, or if things do not come back into your mind after a while. The most important thing for a diagnosis of dementia is finding that your memory has deteriorated. This is a change that you would witness over perhaps 1 or 2, or even 3 years, rather than a general observation that your memory is not as good as it was, say, 20 years ago. It is also important to remember that the majority of older people do not have dementia.

Is it necessary to tell the difference between the different types of dementia?

Some people say that there is no particular need to know whether someone has Alzheimer's disease or vascular dementia, dementia with Lewy bodies or any of the other different types of dementia. Their point is that dementia is an incurable disease for which nothing can be done so it makes no difference to know the exact cause. However, this is no longer the case.

There are now many good reasons why it is necessary to have an accurate diagnosis of the cause of dementia. The new anti-dementia drugs are licensed specifically for the treatment of mild to moderate Alzheimer's disease and to gain benefit from these drugs, an accurate diagnosis is necessary. When one is trying to predict what will happen in the future, it is also important to know which type of dementia an individual suffers from. People with vascular dementia tend to have an episodic and fluctuating course whereas those with Alzheimer's disease tend to have a more gradual decline.

In some situations where the dementia runs in families, other family members will find it useful to know the exact kind of dementia from which a relative suffers. In dementia with Lewy bodies, certain types of drug need to be avoided as they can give rise to symptoms of Parkinson's disease. Finally, for the purpose of learning more about dementia and its causes it is important to have an accurate diagnosis if someone is taking part in a research study.

The doctors have asked if a post-mortem can be carried out when my husband dies. He suffers from Alzheimer's disease. Why is this and what should I say?

To be absolutely certain of a diagnosis of a cause of dementia, the brain needs to be examined in detail under a microscope. In this way, it is no different to any other branch of medicine, where a definitive diagnosis of the condition is made by the examination of an organ or piece of tissue. Examinations and investigations during life are the practical way in which a diagnosis is made. If one has a lump on the skin or a lump in a breast, some tissue is taken away during life. It is impractical, and sometimes dangerous to do a brain biopsy, which would be the only way of looking at a piece of the brain before someone has died.

By asking for a post-mortem examination, the doctors would, in a sense, be able to test out the accuracy of their diagnosis and learn from that and teach others to make a more and more accurate diagnosis on individual patients. The important thing to remember is that to examine a piece of brain under the microscope means that the brain has to be kept, sometimes completely, sometimes parts of it, after the person has died. The whole brain would not be buried with the body. The person asking for the post-mortem examination will be able to give you full details of what happens locally and what tests and investigations would be carried out. Sometimes, if a death occurs in suspicious circumstances and/or the person has not been seen by a doctor recently, a coroner's post-mortem examination is carried out.

As to whether to agree to the examination or not, this is a matter of absolute personal choice and no-one can make you agree to the examination. Some people are governed by what the person would have said themselves before they developed the disease – some people take the view that they will do anything they can to help science – even after they are dead. Others say that they do not want to be messed around. Some religions do not allow such examinations as they feel it amounts to a desecration of the body. In the end, it is a matter of personal choice. The reason the doctors have asked before the person has died is that some people consider that to ask for a post-mortem examination at the time of death is insensitive because of the upset of the bereavement. It is often better to make a decision well in advance of death and to prepare yourself for it. In some research projects the individual is asked to agree to a post-mortem examination at a time when they understand what is happening and are well able to make an informed and valid decision.

What are the risk factors for developing Alzheimer's disease?

We know that Alzheimer's disease becomes commoner as we get older. It occurs in people suffering from Down's syndrome and in some families it is genetic. Other risk factors include a head injury (some people say that professional footballers are more prone to developing Alzheimer's disease because they repeatedly head the ball and boxers develop a form of dementia called dementia pugilistica, which results from repeated head injury), an episode of depression earlier in life and medical illnesses such as hypothyroidism. There is also some evidence that people with a poor education are more prone to the development of Alzheimer's disease. The risk factors for vascular dementia include being overweight, smoking, having high cholesterol, having uncontrolled diabetes and high blood pressure. There is no evidence that smoking is protective against Alzheimer's disease. There is some evidence that taking oestrogens and some pain-killing drugs may help to protect against the development of Alzheimer's disease.

Can water on the brain cause dementia?

The brain is bathed in a fluid called cerebrospinal fluid. The fluid is made in the middle of the brain and is drained to the surface of the brain and then down the spinal cord where it is absorbed. If there is a blockage to the normal circulation of the fluid, it results in a build-up in the inside of the head and the brain is effectively squashed against the skull and flattened. In children, if this happens before the skull bones have fused, then the head expands. In adults, this does not happen.

If there is some damage to the circulation of the fluid in adults, the brain is squashed against the skull and can give rise to some characteristic symptoms. These can include dementia, incontinence of urine quite early on in the illness (it is quite common to be incontinent but in Alzheimer's disease and other dementias this tends to occur later in the illness), trouble with walking, and characteristically walking with a wide-based step. Diagnosis is made on a brain scan. In some situations, diverting the fluid from the middle of the brain through a plastic tube into the heart or abdomen can greatly reduce the effects of the pressure and symptoms can improve.

Can alcohol cause dementia?

There is no doubt that drinking excess alcohol is very damaging to your health and can result in a lot of physical problems. It is usually apparent when taking a history that someone's dementia is caused by excess alcohol intake. There is some evidence that if a person stops drinking completely, then some of the signs and symptoms of dementia may improve or at the very least do not deteriorate. There is also some evidence that drinking red wine can be protective against the development of Alzheimer's disease but, as with most things, it is best to pursue the maxim 'moderation in all things'. Generally, it is recommended not to drink more than 21 units a week for women and 28 units a week for men (1 unit = a measure of spirits, a glass of wine or half a pint of normal strength beer).

My husband has been diagnosed as having dementia but we are worried it is Creutzfeldt–Jakob disease. Is there a test for this?

Creutzfeldt–Jakob disease is a severe form of dementia that has been in the news recently because it has affected a number of very young people. The hallmark of Creutzfeldt–Jakob disease (said to be the human form of BSE, bovine spongiform encephalopathy, which affects cattle) is that it is a very severe illness and people are often dead within months or a year or two of their first symptoms. One of the features of the disease is that people develop jerks or muscle spasms. These do occur in people with other types of dementia but tend to occur later in the illness. The diagnosis is usually made on clinical grounds and the appearances of the brain waves (made on an EEG machine) are diagnostic in that they show a particular wave pattern of the electrical activity of the brain. There is a blood test that is available for the definitive diagnosis, which can also be made after death.

Can Parkinson's disease cause dementia?

There seems to be a crossover between Parkinson's disease and one particular type of dementia, dementia with Lewy bodies. People with Parkinson's disease do develop symptoms of dementia such as loss of memory and people with dementia of the Lewy body type can present with some of the signs and symptoms of Parkinson's disease (tremor, stiffness of the muscles and an expressionless face and falls). It is particularly common in this type of dementia to suffer from visual hallucinations (seeing things) and delusional ideas (false ideas out of which the person cannot be argued).

Is it true that dementia can come on after an anaesthetic?

There is increasing evidence that a general anaesthetic can give rise to symptoms of dementia such as loss of memory and disorientation. What may happen is that a general anaesthetic can make people more aware of symptoms of dementia. When an illness comes on gradually, it is very understandable to try and tie in the onset of symptoms to a readily identifiable and recognisable event such as having an operation. It is not unusual for relatives to say that they have noticed a deterioration since the person had an operation. However, more studies need to be done to make a definitive link between memory loss, dementia and anaesthetics.

What is the link between Down's syndrome and Alzheimer's disease?

People with Down's syndrome develop the changes in the brain of Alzheimer's disease when they are in their middle forties (this has been discovered by doing brain examinations when people with Down's syndrome die prematurely). Down's syndrome sufferers have three copies of chromosome 21 (instead of the normal two). It is not clear why people with Down's syndrome develop Alzheimer's disease.

My husband has some memory problems and has been referred to a 'memory clinic'. Why is that and what are they likely to do?

Memory clinics are a fairly recent development in the National Health Service. They are specialist outpatient clinics set up specifically to diagnose and often treat people complaining of memory problems. They have the ability to investigate, diagnose and treat people suffering from a whole range of psychiatric and physical conditions, which can give rise to memory problems. It is likely that your husband will be seen by a number of different specialists and will have detailed memory tests and a physical examination. It is also likely that he will have some investigations such as a computed tomography (CT) scan and an electroencephalogram (EEG) so that his brain waves can be studied. It is important that he and you are told the results of all these tests and examinations, that you are given a diagnosis, and are provided with details about follow-up. This may include one or more of the following:

• a course of treatment for a physical condition (such as hypothyroidism);
• a course of treatment for depression (drugs and/or counselling);
• some practical advice about how to improve his memory; or
• reassurance that his memory is normal and that there is nothing to worry about.

In some situations, it is not clear what the diagnosis is and it may be that he would be asked to come to the hospital again for repeat tests in a few months time.

My wife has dementia. Can I take her abroad on holiday?

Many people with dementia can travel around the country or abroad without any difficulties provided that someone travels with them. Indeed, despite a diagnosis of dementia, life goes on and it is important and pleasurable to visit new places or to attend family events. However, some people with dementia find travelling outside familiar places challenging, disorienting, or distressing.

If the person with dementia is often agitated or disoriented in familiar places, or if on short trips they usually ask to go home, if they get anxious around other people or if they have behaviours which are hard to handle, then travelling long distances should be approached with a degree of caution. It may be a good idea to try a test trip to somewhere nearer to home to see how that person responds but if this is not possible it would be wise to develop a contingency plan for when travelling. Such a plan would include:

• remembering to pack medication in hand luggage;
• finding out about health services in other countries;
• taking your doctor's phone number with you;
• making sure you both wear identity bracelets;
• using stopovers to break up the journey;
• letting travel guides or airline staff know if you are having problems.

Travel insurance may be more expensive – it is always best to check this point as keeping information from an insurer may make a subsequent claim invalid.

My husband gets more confused and restless every evening. Why is this?

This is quite common and is often termed the 'sundown syndrome'. During the late afternoon or early evening, a person with dementia can become more demanding, distressed, suspicious, or disoriented than at other times of the day. The reason why this occurs is uncertain but it may be that the person is tired and less able to deal with what is going on around them or it may be that the loss of daytime cues (daylight, seeing the postman pass, etc.) makes it harder to orient themselves. Everything becomes more of a challenge and the often-fragile connection to reality can be severed and the person's behaviour can reflect a desperate attempt to regain a sense of security or familiarity.

My wife keeps crying and asking for her mother who died many years ago. I have to constantly remind her of this but she just gets more upset. Why is this?

Asking repetitive questions is not uncommon and can be a major source of frustration for the carer. Sometimes the person's memory difficulties cause them to repeat themselves. Some may be bored and use it to get a response from others and sometimes the person may not have heard the answer to a question.

The context of the question being asked is important and may reveal an unmet need. Asking for 'mother' may imply that person is looking for security, comfort, or affection. It may be that due to disorientation they are reliving a memory of a time when mother was still alive and are naturally enquiring as to where she is.

Trying to reorient the person to the loss of a loved one can be harsh and counterproductive, forcing them repeatedly to grieve for a loved one whilst not stopping the questioning from happening. If anything it may induce a greater need for comfort or reassurance, which may be further expressed through the repetitive question. It may be more appropriate to offer support and to make use of validation therapy, which was mentioned earlier in this book.

My husband suffers from dementia and I am worried that he is still driving. What can I do if he refuses to give up?

The issue of driving and dementia is a very common problem and will become more so as people who are regular car users get older. Not everyone with dementia is banned from driving, but clearly, if a person has a severe degree of cognitive impairment it is inappropriate and dangerous for them to do so. In this situation, the rights of the individual to drive are outweighed by the risk to others. If your husband has been given a diagnosis of dementia, he must inform the DVLA about it (you or any member of your family can do this on his behalf). It is the DVLA that decides after taking advice from your GP and any specialists involved in your husband's care.

It is often very difficult to try to persuade someone to stop driving if they enjoy it and, as is often the case, they see no reason why they should stop. Try and talk to your husband, saying that the law says he must report the matter to the DVLA. If he does not, he will be driving without insurance and the consequences of an accident could be very serious indeed. Your GP and others (e.g. a son-in-law) may be of help. It rarely comes to the situation where a relative has to hide the car keys or disable the car, but occasionally this is necessary. The important thing to emphasise is that the decision about driving is not yours or your GP's, it is the authorities at the DVLC who decide.

My mother has early dementia and I would like to take over the handling of her financial affairs. How do I go about this?

There are a number of options which may be appropriate to gain some control over your mother's financial affairs. If she is still able to understand the implications of giving you power to pay her bills and help with her finances (try and avoid the idea that you are taking over control), an Enduring Power of Attorney is the appropriate way forward. A solicitor can arrange this for you. If she has lost this ability, then you should apply to the Court of Protection (she needs to have assets of over £5000 for this to be used). A doctor completes a certificate and the Court gives someone (usually the applicant) the power to handle financial affairs.

6 CASE STUDIES

These case studies are made up from the authors' clinical experience. They do not relate to real patients but are an amalgamation of some of the common symptoms from which people may suffer and are presented to illustrate some of the important points when considering the diagnosis and management of someone complaining of a memory problem. Each case is followed by a comment.

Case 1: depression can give rise to symptoms of memory loss

A 75-year-old woman went to see her GP complaining of memory problems. She described how over the last 6 months she had noticed that she had begun to forget things. The examples she gave were her daughter's birthday, her grandson's christening and her sister's wedding anniversary. This was unusual for her as she usually prided herself at having a good memory. She felt her memory was getting worse although she had noticed that it varied from day to day. She was generally fit and healthy. She had had a past history of depression treated with antidepressants by her GP many years ago. Her husband had died suddenly of a heart attack the previous year and it was approaching the first anniversary of his death.

On questioning, she said that she had had some trouble sleeping over the past few months and was tending to wake up earlier in the morning than usual. At times she felt sad and had begun to cry when she saw pictures of her husband in the bedroom. This surprised her as she felt she had got over his death. She said that occasionally she had felt like taking her time when crossing the road so that a bus could run her over and surprised herself by not being upset by these thoughts. Her appetite was good. Her daughter had noticed that she had become more irritable with her grandchildren, on whom she generally doted.

On examination she scored well on a test of her memory but her GP thought she was depressed. He prescribed a course of antidepressants. She was reassured that he did not think her memory problems were severe and that she was not 'going mad' and that the drugs were not addictive.

When she was seen again by her GP 3 months later, she was bright and happy and said her memory had almost completely returned to normal. Her family had spontaneously said that they felt she was a lot better. Her GP persuaded her to take her antidepressants for a further 12 months and when seen at that time she had returned completely to her normal self.

Depression can often present as memory problems. The secret here was to suspect that she may have been depressed and then to ask more questions. The clues are:
- the history was quite short for someone with a dementia (usually, but not always, the symptoms are present for a year or more);
- she complained of the problems herself (often, but not always, people with dementia tend to lose insight early in the illness and are brought to the doctor's attention by family members;
- she has a past history of depression (this seems to be a risk factor for the development of Alzheimer's disease as well as giving a clue that depression may be the diagnosis);
- she had several of the classical features of depression (sleep disturbance with early morning wakening, irritability and thoughts of ending her life).

Case 2: a brain tumour

A 63-year-old man was referred to hospital by his GP. For the past 3 months he had complained of loss of memory for specific events. He had forgotten an important appointment at work and had forgotten to go to the dentist, even though it was in his diary. He said that he was eating and sleeping well and had no symptoms suggestive of depression. He had been previously fit and well although he had been treated for asthma for a number of years. He said that he had been able to cover up his lapses of memory so none of his relatives or friends had noticed anything. He had given a couple of possible excuses for the forgotten appointments. He noticed that his memory loss tended to vary from day to day – if he forgot something it invariably came back to him a few days later.

On questioning, he said that he had felt more tired in the last 6 weeks or so. He complained of a feeling of fuzziness in his head and some headaches, which were worse in the morning. He also said he felt sick in the morning and on two occasions had vomited. He described some tingling down the left side of his body, which he had experienced on two occasions for about half an hour each. He said he was very conscious of memory problems because he was currently looking after his mother who had recently been diagnosed as having Alzheimer's disease and loss of memory was among her initial symptoms.

On examination, his reflexes were increased on the right side of his body (demonstrated by a increased muscle jerk reaction when his elbow, wrist and knee joints were tapped with a tendon hammer). He seemed to have some loss of sensation on the skin down the right-hand side. A CT scan was performed, which showed he had a brain tumour on the left side of the brain (because the brain and the body tend to be crossed over, i.e. the left side of the brain controls the right side of the body and vice versa, this would explain the symptoms). He was referred to a brain surgeon for an operation and the tumour was successfully treated.

Comment
It is very rare for people to have brain tumours but they do occur. The suspicious symptoms in this case were that the symptoms had only been present for a few weeks and the person's physical symptoms were suggestive of raised pressure in the head, i.e. a headache which was worse in the morning and was associated with sickness. A brain scan is the only way of diagnosing a brain tumour and the treatment is usually by surgery, by chemotherapy (drugs) or by radiotherapy (x-ray treatment). The fact that his mother suffered from Alzheimer's disease probably made him come forward sooner than he might have otherwise. The variability in memory loss and the fact that memories did return eventually would be unusual for someone with dementia.

Case 3: a stroke causing symptoms of dementia

An old age psychiatrist was asked to see a 78-year-old woman at home, having been called there by her son who lived nearby. The story was that the woman's husband had died 3 years previously and she lived on her own but had good support from her son and from her daughter-in-law, to whom she was very close. She had been able to look after herself well and had enjoyed an active social life with her friend, going to a luncheon club twice a week and going to her friend's to play bridge.

All of a sudden, 6 weeks ago, she had an episode described by her son as one of confusion. She rang up about 7 o'clock one evening (she did this three or four times a week anyway) and started to call him by her dead husband's name. She did not seem to know exactly what was happening and was unclear why she had rung. Her son and daughter-in-law were very concerned and went round immediately. They noticed that her speech seemed a little slurred and they thought she was leaning more to the right side. She was able to recognise her son and daughter-in-law and clearly appreciated that her husband had died. They had not seen her for a couple of days and it was clear that she had not done the dishes or tidied up since they had last seen her. She seemed rather restless and was unable to sit down. They were so concerned that they decided to stay with her overnight. By the next morning she was back to her normal self. She clearly had little recollection of having telephoned the previous day and seemed surprised when she woke up and found her son and daughter-in-law there.

A fortnight later, a similar incident occurred. She 'phoned her son at work in the late afternoon asking him what he wanted for his tea that evening. When he explained that he did not usually come round for his tea (but said he would be happy to do so if she wanted), she became very angry at him, accusing him of having left home without discussing it with her. She slammed the 'phone down on him. He went round that evening and found her to be completely normal. There was no evidence of slurring of speech and she was not leaning to the right-hand side any more.

Her GP carried out a number of physical tests. He found her pulse and blood pressure to be normal and a general medical examination (lungs, heart and abdomen) were also normal. There was no evidence to suggest any weakness down one side or the other which would be consistent with a stroke. Her GP had known her and her husband for a number of years and knew that she had been physically well throughout her life.

He referred her to the local old age psychiatry department. A CT scan was ordered which showed she had had two strokes.

Comment

This lady has clearly suffered from the effects of a stroke. The fact that the onset of her confusion was very sudden and short-lived and was associated with two symptoms which occur commonly as a result of stroke (slurring of speech and leaning to one side) strongly suggest that that is the main cause of her symptoms. The fact that evidence of a stroke was found in a brain scan confirms this but it is important to note that finding an area of damage on a brain scan is very common and can occur in the absence of any symptoms. There was no evidence, before the episode of confusion and memory loss that she was not able to manage her affairs and this strongly suggests that there is no dementia. There is no specific treatment for a stroke but there are a number of things that can be done which seem to reduce significantly the chances of having a second stroke. These may include the prescription of a small dose of aspirin a day and making sure that other risk factors are kept under control, e.g. to avoid being overweight, to stop smoking and to control medical conditions such as high blood pressure and diabetes.

Case 4: middle-age stress

A 42-year-old man presented to his general practitioner with a 9-month history of memory loss. He said that he had been under increasing strain at work and has been passed over recently for a promotion in favour of a younger man. He had begun to feel frustrated at his job and at life in general. He had suffered three panic attacks and had begun to get palpitations and butterflies in his stomach. All his friends told him he was working too hard. He had taken up smoking again (having not smoked for 20 years) and was drinking much more alcohol than he used to. He sometimes found it difficult to sleep at night. He was eating well and his sex drive was unchanged.

On examination, he had symptoms of anxiety but there was no evidence of depression (he enjoyed things, felt no guilt, was looking forward to the future and was able to take pleasure in things).

He was referred to a neuropsychologist for detailed tests of his memory. These were all entirely normal. A diagnosis was made of stress-induced memory impairment. He was given a course of cognitive behaviour therapy and when seen 6 months later he was completely recovered.

Comment

Increasingly, memory complaints are seen in people who clearly are under stress. This is something that is a common experience — if we have a great deal to think about, it is easy to forget things. The important things in the situation described above is to reassure the individual that he does not have Alzheimer's disease and, also, that there are no signs of depression. A psychological approach to the management of this individual is the most appropriate and the prescription of a sedative drug or antidepressant is inappropriate. In extreme situations, a drug can be given (called a beta-blocker), which can diminish some of the physical symptoms and anxiety such as the palpitations and butterflies in the stomach. The person should realize that he is suffering from stress and it is only through that self-recognition that a person can get better.

Case 5: a physical illness

A 68-year-old woman went to see her general practitioner because of a number of symptoms. These were:
- tiredness, which had come on over the last year;
- loss of memory for recent events (she had forgotten a couple of appointments with her friend);
- weight gain (about a stone over the last 6 months without an increase in her appetite);
- concerns that her hair was falling out; and
- a dislike of the cold (she found that she had to put on an extra jumper when she went out).

Her GP did some blood tests and found her to have an underactive thyroid. She was given replacement treatment and when seen 6 months later she was completely well.

Comment

It is not unusual for symptoms of memory loss to accompany symptoms of a physical illness such as an underactivity of the thyroid gland. It is important to ask about other symptoms that may indicate if there is a physical illness alongside complaints of memory problems. Most physical illnesses can be diagnosed fairly easily by a medical examination and an investigation such as a blood test.

Case 6: confusional state

An 89-year-old woman was asked to come and see her GP by her social worker. She had been suffering from arthritis for a number of years and while the pain she suffered from her joints was controlled with pain killers, she had needed quite a lot of help around the house to adapt her living accommodation to her physical disabilities. For example, she needed a rail to help her get in and out of the bath and needed a raised toilet seat because it was very painful for her to sit on a low chair.

Her social worker was concerned because she had noticed several lapses of concentration in her client. The lady never complained of anything and had a very stoical outlook on life. Her social worker noticed that she had become more breathless over the last few months and at these times had appeared to become much more disorientated and confused. She had been neglecting herself and, despite her painful arthritis, was usually very neat and tidy and kept the house clean. The house had become noticeably more dirty and grimy – the lady had always refused the offer of a home help. At her worst, she did not know the day or the time and had no idea of the date. She often did not know where she was and sometimes mistook her current flat for one she had lived in many years ago on the other side of the city. She tended to leave the front door open. At her best, she knew exactly the date and time and knew where she was. She was safety conscious and always asked visitors for their identification before letting them into her flat.

A physical examination by her GP revealed that she had swollen ankles and noises could be heard at the back of her chest through a stethoscope. Also, the veins in her neck were very full. This indicated that she had heart failure and this was treated with a diuretic tablet (a tablet which gets rid of excess water from the body) and digoxin (derived from the foxglove – a tablet that increases the strength of the contraction of the heart). Over the next 2 months there were no more episodes of confusion and disorientation and no more signs of breathlessness. She went back to her usual self and her house returned to its usual state of cleanliness and tidiness.

Comment

This lady suffered from a physical illness (heart failure) which temporarily upset her brain function and gave her symptoms similar to dementia, i.e. disorientation to time and place, self-neglect and a poor short-term memory. It is common in people as they get older to have episodes of physical illness and any physical problem can give rise to a confusional state. The most common are episodes of heart failure, a urinary tract infection, or a chest infection. Some more serious illnesses such as cancer can also be associated with episodes of confusion. The management is to treat the underlying illness and the signs and symptoms usually resolve a few days or a few weeks later.

7 TEN WAYS TO IMPROVE YOUR MEMORY

1. DON'T PANIC! Allow yourself the time to bring the information back. It doesn't matter if it is a little slower.
2. Try to imagine where you were when you first heard or saw the information that you are trying to recall. Put yourself back in the same context as vividly as possible.
3. Pen and paper are the most useful tools to aid your memory. If your memory is not so good, write things down. Do this for even fairly mundane things because when someone asks you what you did yesterday, you can come up with an answer, rather than 'I can't remember', which is not helpful for your confidence. Diaries work well because they can help you to organise information and also keep you in touch with days and dates.
4. Try to 'muster up' all your concentration when carrying out an activity or information that you may be liable to forget. Try to repeat the information back to yourself from time to time, e.g. 'her name is Catherine'.
5. Combine a visual image with words, for example, 'her name is Catherine and she has curly hair'.
6. Keep everything in its place as far as is possible. For example, keys and spectacles are easy to misplace, so put them down in the same place whenever you can. Again, when you put them down try to 'visualise' the place in order to jog your memory. For example, if you put your keys onto a specific table, imagine the table carved into the shape of a giant key. The more humorous and larger than life the image, the more likely you are to remember it.
7. If you need to take certain objects with you when going out, for example, an umbrella, put it in front of the door, maybe on the mat. You would have to step over it anyway to go out, and would then see it and remember it.
8. Use 'post it' notes in prominent places, for example, near the cooker or on the back of the kitchen door – 'SWITCH OFF COOKER', 'PUT LIGHTS OUT'. Cupboards can also be labelled with the names of the objects that go inside.
9. Go through the alphabet if you need to remember a name or word.
10. Be honest! 'My memory is not as good as it used to be' will often take the pressure off you, and many people can relate to this. Everyone recognises that you have to adapt your life if you have a sore back, or a hip replacement, or diabetes, and it is just the same with having a poor memory. Most older people will experience some decline in their memory, and almost everyone will have had instances during a lifetime when their memory has been less than perfect.

APPENDIX USEFUL ADDRESSES

Alzheimer's Society
Gordon House
10 Greencoat Place
London SW1P 1PH
Tel: 020 7306 0606
Fax: 020 7306 0808
Helpline: 0845 300 0336
Website: www.alzheimers.org.uk

Alzheimer Scotland -
Action on Dementia
22 Drumsheugh Gardens
Edinburgh
EH3 7RN
Tel: 0131 243 1453
Fax: 0131 243 1450
Helpline: 0808 808 3000
E-mail: alzheimer@alzscot.org

CANDID (Counselling and Diagnosis in
Dementia)
The National Hospital for Neurology and
Neurosurgery
Queen Square
London WC1N 3BG
Tel: 020 7829 8772
Fax: 020 7209 0182

Parkinson's Disease Society
United Scientific House
215 Vauxhall Bridge Road
London SW1V 1EJ
Tel: 020 7931 8080
Fax: 020 7233 9908
Helpline: 020 7233 5373

Age Concern England
Astral House
1268 London Road
London SW16 4ER
Tel: 020 8765 7200

Age Concern Scotland
113 Rose Street
Edinburgh
EH2 3DT
Tel: 0131 220 3345

Association of Crossroads Care Attendants
ANTS Schemes
10 Regent Place
Rugby
Warwickshire CV21 2PN
Tel: 01788 573653

The Carers National Association
20-25 Glasshouse Yard
London EC1A 4JS
Tel: 020 7490 8818
Helpline: 020 7490 8898

Creutzfeldt-Jakob Disease Support
Network
Alzheimer's Society
Gordon House
10 Greencoat Place
London SW1 1PH
Tel: 020 7306 0606
Fax: 020 7306 0808
Helpline: 0845 300 0336
Website: www.alzheimers.org.uk

The Public Trust Office (For legal advice,
Court of Protection)
Stuart House
24 Kingsway
London WC2B 6JX
Tel: 0207 664 7300

INDEX